T0305206

Democracy's Hidden Heroes

Democracy's Hidden Heroes

Fitting Policy to People and Place

David C. Campbell

TEMPLE UNIVERSITY PRESS
Philadelphia • Rome • Tokyo

TEMPLE UNIVERSITY PRESS
Philadelphia, Pennsylvania 19122
tupress.temple.edu

Copyright © 2024 by Temple University—Of The Commonwealth System
   of Higher Education
All rights reserved
Published 2024

Library of Congress Cataloging-in-Publication Data

Names: Campbell, David Coleman, 1956– author.
Title: Democracy's hidden heroes : fitting policy to people and place /
   David C. Campbell.
Description: Philadelphia : Temple University Press, 2024. | Includes
   bibliographical references and index. | Summary: "Tells the stories of
   public managers, nonprofit directors, and other local leaders who turn
   deeply rooted governance dilemmas into practical policy results, and
   examines what these stories can teach us about governance and democratic
   agency"— Provided by publisher.
Identifiers: LCCN 2023033013 (print) | LCCN 2023033014 (ebook) | ISBN
   9781439924587 (paperback) | ISBN 9781439924570 (cloth) | ISBN
   9781439924594 (pdf)
Subjects: LCSH: Community-based social services—California—Case studies.
   | Human services $z California—Management—Case studies. | Human
   services personnel—California—Case studies. | Nonprofit
   organizations—Government policy—California—Case studies. |
   Interorganizational relations—California—Case studies. | BISAC:
   POLITICAL SCIENCE / Public Policy / Social Policy | POLITICAL SCIENCE /
   Public Affairs & Administration
Classification: LCC HV66 .C367 2024 (print) | LCC HV66 (ebook) | DDC
   361.309794—dc23/eng/20240110
LC record available at https://lccn.loc.gov/2023033013
LC ebook record available at https://lccn.loc.gov/2023033014

♾ The paper used in this publication meets the requirements of
the American National Standard for Information Sciences—Permanence of Paper
for Printed Library Materials, ANSI Z39.48-1992

Printed in the United States of America

9 8 7 6 5 4 3 2 1

For the hidden heroes
who redeem the troubled, essential marriage
of metrics and mētis

Contents

Acknowledgments

This book leans heavily on the work of research teams I led or co-led between the mid-1990s and 2021. The teams conducted studies that included more than 2,000 interviews and hundreds of meeting observations from two-thirds of California's fifty-eight counties. Without the state and local stakeholders who graciously shared reflections in open-ended interviews, there would be no story to tell. And without the tireless fieldwork and thoughtful insights of my team members, the story would be decidedly less compelling.

A few colleagues deserve special mention. Much of my research was conducted jointly with Joan Wright. Joan's tireless work ethic and willingness to let her younger colleague garner most of the credit were generous beyond my ability to repay. She introduced me to Cathy Lemp, who was a vital collaborator on many projects. Cathy skillfully performed hundreds of interviews, produced vivid meeting observations, drafted numerous evaluation reports, and shared fearlessly candid feedback that invariably clarified my own thinking. Jim Grieshop and Al Sokolow helped me make a home in the Community Development program at the University of California, Davis, while providing exemplary models of applied scholarship.

Working against the grain of his own organization, Eric Glunt embraced my qualitative approach to policy evaluation and guided me through the labyrinthine nooks and crannies of the California Employment Development Department. Nancy Erbstein and Ned Spang provided essential leadership on projects later in my career, introducing me to fields of study that I could never have navigated on my own. Finally, my longtime colleague Gail Feenstra was responsible for helping me land my first job in Cooperative Extension, with the University of California Sustainable Agriculture Research and Education Program (SAREP). Gail's community food systems research and extension provides an outstanding model of engaged scholarship linking university and community. Working with all these colleagues and friends has been a joy.

I am also grateful to my late colleagues Bob Pence and Ted Bradshaw. Bob contributed his perceptive listening skills and deep insight to multiple projects. Ted helped me secure two major evaluation contracts early in my career, launching the trajectory of applied research that this book recounts. The untimely deaths of both men left major voids.

Many projects benefited from partnerships with colleagues in local Cooperative Extension offices. These University of California academics provided important insights into local history and community context. In some cases, they engaged directly in fieldwork. Among those who contributed were Ann Brosnahan, Gloria Brown, Rebecca Carver, Deb Giraud, Faye Lee, Richard Mahacek, Pat Margolis, Fe Moncloa, Shelley Murdock, Carole Paterson, Sue Pierce, John Pusey, Yvonne Ricketts, Marilyn Rotnem, Anne Sanchez, Estella West, and Martha Weston. Former graduate and postdoctoral students—who now hold leadership positions in academia, government, and nonprofit organizations—also made important contributions, including Ildi Carlisle-Cummins, Lisceth Cruz Carrasco, Wendy Carter, James Fabionar, Anne Gillman, Robin Kozloff, Jean Lamming, Rong Liu, Courtney Marshall, Kelsey Meagher, Kim Nalder, Lisa Nelson, Heather Paulsen, Jonna Reeder, Kristen Rosenow, Sarna Salzman, Rebecca Stark, Jeanette Treiber, and Whitney Wilcox.

Several of our projects featured interviews or focus groups with non-English speakers. I am grateful to the many individuals who conducted or translated these, including Mary Burroughs, Jennifer

Denton, Sandra Franco, Yolanda Rojas, Claudia Sandoval, Gabriel Terronez, Choua Thao, Linda Vang, Sua Vang, Gloria Widner, Bonnie Wilson, Chue Xiong, Leslie Xiong, MyYing Xiong, and Xue Xiong. Other important research collaborators included Dan Ihara, Juliet King, and Sommer Mateu. UC Davis staff who provided key support services included Jeff Woled, Starla Speich, and Leanne Friedman. Carol Hinkle deserves special mention for the countless hours she spent transcribing taped interviews.

Funding support came from the University of California, government agencies, and private foundations. California state agency funders included the Employment Development Department, the Labor and Workforce Development Agency, and the Department of Social Services. Foundation funders included the California Endowment, David and Lucile Packard, James Irvine, Peninsula Community, Miriam and Peter Haas, Walter and Elise Haas, and Sierra Health.

Bernadette Tarallo and Dennis Pendleton are the type of dear friends I could call on to read multiple drafts of the book manuscript, providing encouragement when I most needed it. Lehn Benjamin, my coauthor on one of the articles on which the book draws, provided important advice that led to a significant shift in how I have framed the book's argument. My brother, Jim Campbell, helped me widen the aperture to consider ways the hidden hero stories might speak to a broader audience. I would count the book a success if he and others working at the interface of bureaucracy and community see their efforts reflected in respectful and illuminating terms. Others whose comments and advice have been helpful include Harry Boyte, Leslie Cooksey, Albert Dzur, Nancy Erbstein, Ryan Galt, John Hess, Erica Kohl-Arenas, Bill Lacy, Jonathon London, Scott Peters, Oren Rawls, Carmen Sirianni, Kim Walker, and Bob Wineburg. Aaron Javsicas and colleagues at Temple University Press provided generous support and sound advice as the book neared publication.

At a critical juncture, Dale Hess helped me locate the spine of the book's argument and just as importantly helped me see what did not belong. Much earlier, Dale changed my life as a college student by scratching an itch I did not know I had. Dan Goldrich nurtured me through a Ph.D. in political science while providing an example of a scholar committed to democracy, equity, and sustainability. For preparing me to be ready for what Dale and Dan had to give, I give thanks to an amazing set of social studies teachers in Ridgewood, New Jersey: Miss Schoen, Miss Gold, Mr. Chmel, and Mrs. Haberland. They had me thinking like a social scientist before I knew what that meant. I am particularly grateful to Charlotte Schoen, whose powerful, unorthodox teaching methods kept hope alive in my young soul during a sixth-grade year bookended by my younger sister's death and the assassinations of Martin Luther King Jr. and Bobby Kennedy.

My father was known for his entertaining, seemingly improbable stories and for his ability to engage others in ways that revealed something important. My mother combined the discipline of an English teacher with a passion for young children and social justice. I can only hope that the lasting marks of their spirit and skills are as obvious to my readers as they are to me.

I have a keen respect for the magic that can happen in a well-conducted interview. I met my wife, Mary Lynn Tobin, while interviewing for the student staff of the Westminster College Dean of the Chapel. The active listening skills that Judd McConnell taught to us as staff volunteers have provided sustenance for the long haul, without which I would not have been blessed with either a research career or a fruitful marriage now in its fifth decade.

Democracy's Hidden Heroes

I

The Governance Setting

1

Introduction

Embracing Contraries to Create Results

This book is about the elusive quest to bring about and document the policy results we intend. It is also necessarily about the tension between competing approaches to achieving results, one emphasizing bureaucratic standardization and the other adaptive public management. Most importantly it is about the people who must reconcile these contraries in everyday practice, doing what they can to move the governance process forward—people like Maricela.

As the "navigator" hired by a local workforce development agency, Maricela works at the intersection of the nation's Department of Labor bureaucracy and a community network of youth-serving agencies.[1] The federal agency distributes taxpayer dollars to realize the legislative intent of developing skills in the nation's workforce. The local network links public and nonprofit organizations contracted to implement community-responsive workforce programs for local youth. Maricela's task is aligning the local organizations' wide-ranging activities with bureaucratic resources, results expectations, and compliance demands. Her work is both mundane and highly consequential:

> In our city there is a lot of poverty, a lot of gangs. Our programs help young people succeed despite these circumstances. We

will bring in these kids to talk to the business people on our workforce board. They'll say: "I'm barely eighteen at this point and I've got three kids. I've been in jail; I've been whatever." And then they say: "This program really straightened me out. This program got me my education. This program got me a job. This program did this, that, and the other thing for me." And the business folks are sitting there with their mouths open. They can't help but be moved . . . it's very powerful. It really, really is.

It is the kind of result that both federal officials and local leaders can applaud. Making it happen, however, requires reconciling their contrasting and often incompatible ways of doing business. The bureaucrats rely on universal rules, standard operating procedures, and strict results accountability metrics to steer and control. By contrast, local organizations pride themselves on creative flexibility and nimbleness, crafting emergent strategies that take into account the capacities of different youth-serving organizations and the unique needs and circumstances of individual youth.

Maricela's job was to mesh these distinct organizational cultures, equally necessary yet not easily combined. She notes:

I understand there needs to be accountability. There needs to be proof as to how we're using the money and what the money is doing. But there has to be a better and easier way. When you read all the DOL [Department of Labor] terminology and the big ol' regs, it's like, "Who wrote this? And for whom did you guys write this?" First of all, none of us are lawyers, none of us understand your terminology, and you throw out this big, fat book of [laughs] dos and don'ts. We're like, "Huh? What are we supposed to do with this?"

I don't think the people that write it have any clue as to what is happening at the grassroots, what it takes to actually implement these. It seems that sometimes we're focused more on trying to learn the performance measures, and the criteria, and the eligibility, and collecting documentation, and writing the paperwork than we are on serving the population. You've got DOL people; they don't run programs, and they don't deal with kids; they're just up there going, "Oh, this looks really good on paper." And they have no idea if it's practical or if it's going to work or not.

Frustration with bureaucratic inundation is nothing new. At one time or another, most of us have experienced situations that have provoked rants similar to Maricela's. These experiences with how well-intentioned policies translate into onerous rules at the ground level lend potency to political appeals to deregulate or shrink the size of the government. On the other hand, "those DOL people" know that continued federal funding for local workforce programs depends on documenting performance and on rooting out errors or corruption. The "big ol' regs" locals lament are part of the results accountability currency needed to convince cost-conscious and embarrassment-averse agency heads and legislators, who in turn reflect a public that is increasingly skeptical of what their tax dollars are buying.[2]

Maricela confronts a maddeningly circular dilemma: documenting performance and complying with regulations is at once mission critical and a time swamp that undermines the ability of local organizations to produce intended results. The local Workforce Investment Board created her position to reconcile these competing claims. Just before she was hired, they had created a tightly linked network of six youth-serving organizations. Rather than requiring each of the six contracted providers to satisfy all ten performance elements required by federal workforce legislation, they had carefully chosen organizations to enhance the performance of the network as a whole. Maricela ensures that the entire network collectively meets the ten required results metrics, rather than each contractor individually:

Organizing as a network let everybody do what they're best at, and it was better for the kids, any way you look at it. Today everybody's cooperating, versus competition. As the navigator, I do the dirty work, behind the scenes, like keeping everybody on track in terms of performance. Or other nitty-gritty stuff like reminding providers that even if a youth wasn't eighteen when he came in, if he turns eighteen during the program, you have to sign him up for Selective Service. Little things like that the providers weren't aware of; that's where we come in.

By managing the behind-the-scenes paperwork, Maricela frees the providers to focus attention on the youth they serve rather than on what federal and state auditors require. She notes:

> Let's say one of the six providers enrolls a young person that they find out needs substance-abuse counseling provided by a different organization. They will notify me as the navigator because once you start co-enrolling, there are paperwork nightmares. Because the rules say you can't duplicate services. So I will tell the first organization, "Okay, so they're enrolling the student using this activity code; you're going to enroll them with this [different] activity code." If we remove all the yucky paperwork, then the providers can dedicate their true efforts on serving the client. They are the ones who know when a young person is struggling at school because, more than likely, another young person told them, "Hey, so-and-so's been ditching class." They develop such a rapport with the community that it's truly a grassroot type of service delivery.
>
> Asking providers to take on all the technicalities—labor law, changes to rules and regulations, et cetera—would only distract them from understanding what is going on in the community and with particular youth. They would say: "This is way too much paperwork. This is ridiculous. We want to focus on serving the youth." The workforce bureaucracy is not an easy ticket; it's really very intensive; it can be very overwhelming to a local nonprofit that has never dealt with a federal agency. So I take care of all the bureaucracy, and reminders, and so forth.

It is not that Maricela finds the bureaucratic rules always wrong and the youth providers always right. Instead, she is constantly seeking the right balance, something that takes time and experience to develop:

> The providers, if you let them, they'll say, "Well, it's not raining anywhere; I don't have to do that." Obviously, we're not over their head with a hammer the whole time: "Well, it says it here, you have to be in our meeting." But if we ever have to refer to the rules, we need to cover all our bases. Our very first RFP [request for proposals] could have used a lot of work. It was

very trusting, if you will. We weren't as savvy as we are now, and experienced, working with different providers and issues and so forth. So the RFP has since been beefed up to hold them accountable to do more things.

Note the tightrope Maricela must walk. Too much oversight or too many compliance demands can squelch what makes the nonprofit providers excel: their focus on the youth themselves. Too little oversight and the local network can't meet the federal expectations to which continuing funds are attached, without which the nonprofits can't continue to serve the needs of the community's youth.

How best to walk this tightrope is the type of deeply ingrained governance dilemma this book explores. Before describing that dilemma in general terms, let's consider a second case example, in many ways more typical of the problems found where bureaucracy and community meet and often collide. As difficult as Maricela's work might appear, it represents a best-case scenario in that her job description addresses a problem that is endemic but seldom acknowledged so explicitly. Typically, the work of mediating between state bureaucracies and community networks falls on the shoulders of individuals whose primary job duties lie elsewhere, as in the following example.

Caught between State Standards and Community Capacities

Hideo is the executive director of a nonprofit organization that serves as his county's childcare resource and referral agency. The organization keeps a database of all providers and informs parents where to find childcare that meets their needs. When welfare reform sent thousands of single mothers into the workforce, Hideo's organization faced the challenge of rapidly expanding childcare capacity. As Hideo put it: "We estimate that we are going to be about 27,000 slots short. So we're basically being asked to double our capacity in five years or so." To address this challenge, his strategy was to work with faith communities, taking advantage of their trusted status, dispersed locations, and available space during the work week.

To inform the public, Hideo began to attend community meetings, speaking on the same panels as county welfare officials. From a citizen perspective, he *was* a county official. This became abundantly clear when disgruntled welfare clients who had been kicked off the rolls began issuing death threats to his agency. "We used to be wide open," he laments, "but now we are becoming more like a classic welfare program with a key pass to enter because we've had three or four death threats. Technically we are not an arm of the county as a nonprofit, but the lines are getting blurred. The good side of that is that we now have better working relationships with county staff."

In developing relationships with religious institutions, "we encountered a lot of bumps," says Hideo. "Some of them saw childcare as a way to make money and help their budgets. We had to be very clear: 'you are not going to make money doing this.'" Hideo's team offered detailed workshops for interested churches, walking them through the stringent state licensing requirements. As it turned out, most churches were not able to meet the rigorous standards:

> It seems like every time we get close another issue will come up . . . the playground doesn't meet the specifications, or the heating and air system isn't up to standard and won't get past licensing. This history of this project is that something will always come up. In hindsight, we went about it wrong. There was a lot of pressure in our county to work with the community as welfare reform took place. So we did. We said to congregations: "We have money for this, can you help us?" We didn't really go into the churches and learn about them and help them learn what this would really take. So a lot of them shared the concern about childcare and were willing to help but didn't really have what it took to make it happen.

In this case, there was very little flexibility in terms of bending the state licensing requirements themselves. Hideo himself is a big believer in high standards: "The data has been piling up on the benefits of high-quality childcare," says Hideo. "The requirements are strict to make it more likely that will happen. The difficult part is how to maintain that human contact; you can't run human services like a corporation."

Bringing the state standards into alignment with the culture and capacity of local churches proved in most cases to be a bridge too far. Two years after our first interview with Hideo, he could point to only a few examples where churches were now operating new childcare facilities. "There have been so many barriers," he laments.

Hideo's stance in straddling bureaucratic and community cultures is full of ambiguity. On the question of standards, he sides with the inflexible standards of the state even if it means that very few church childcare facilities are started. But in other comments he praised the community's way of working together while criticizing state officials and practices. "You serve clients; you don't serve the beast. We can get things done here because in our community we can base it on somebody's word. If you've worked with somebody and you know they are going to come through on their promises, you can get started on projects knowing the money or other resources will be there."

By contrast, Hideo found that the state's promises about childcare funding proved to be illusory. "At the beginning they said to families, 'We're going to pay for your childcare as long as you are financially eligible for it.' Now they are saying they never intended to fully fund it." At the time we were speaking, welfare reform provided childcare funding for those enrolled in welfare-to-work programs, but no funding stream supported childcare for the working poor. If welfare-to-work participants succeeded in getting jobs, most of them landed among the working poor and became ineligible for childcare support. This often had the perverse effect of driving them back onto the welfare rolls (Hacker 2004, 253).

"It has been traumatic to say the least," says Hideo. "We've had parents testifying at state hearings. They bare their souls. The testimony actually seems to be fairly successful, because all of a sudden there was an additional set of funds released. But it's just tossing a carrot at us because it's a short-term fix. No one is willing to realize that we have to come up with a system that supports all the working poor, not just those coming off of welfare."

An Important, Neglected Site of Democratic Agency

In sharing stories like the two just recounted, my purpose in this book is to shine a light on an important though neglected site of democratic agency. It is found at the intersection of two different forms and languages, one bureaucratic, hierarchical, and metric-reliant and the other communal, networked, and infused with a nuanced feel for

local assets and limitations. Bureaucratic hierarchies and community networks both seek to realize public intentions through collective action, but they rely on different types of usable knowledge and
make contrasting claims to democratic legitimacy. Their differences
frequently put them at odds, each perceiving as counterproductive what
the other considers a standard way of doing business.

These misgivings are not mirages. However, if that is all they can
see in each other, the two parties are prevented from creating results
that require their combined strengths. This is especially the case in
redressing poverty and repairing the damage it inflicts on individuals and communities. While disadvantaged communities have many
important internal assets (McKnight 1995), they are nonetheless dependent on external resources. These resources typically come in bu-
reaucratically wrapped packages, from either public agencies or private
foundations. A predictable litany of programmatic and administrative dilemmas follows, as public and nonprofit managers struggle to
reconcile the competing ideals of vertical accountability and locally
attuned stakeholder engagement.

Every day in schools, human services departments, workforce development agencies, and similar local organizations, democracy's hidden heroes like Maricela and Hideo endeavor to align universal rules
and top-down compliance demands with the particularities of place
and people, adapting policy and programs to the situation at hand.[3]
Working in a realm of trade-offs and half measures, their efforts are
seldom fully successful. But their humble, persistent way of "embracing contraries" (Elbow 1986) sends a clear message: democratic agency will only flourish if we learn to reconcile the oddly conjoined cultures of centrally managed bureaucracies and communities capable
of purposive, reflective, and contextually appropriate action, thereby
achieving results that neither can achieve on their own.

As an evaluator of collaborative community initiatives funded by
government and large private foundations, I have had unusual access
to the places where this drama of contemporary governance unfolds.
Indeed, I myself have been part of the story, struggling to honor the
diverse voices of the characters and to make sense of the overall plot.
The protagonists—government and foundation funders, on the one
hand, and participants in networks of benevolent community care,
on the other—share the goal of improving the health and well-being

of children, families, and communities. They are partners in a quest to produce tangible results, driven by their own civic motivations and increasingly by accountability demands imposed by others. The funders have the resources and some types of expertise that the community partners need. Network participants have local knowledge without which the funders' initiatives cannot be adapted successfully to place and personal circumstance. If they could find a way to bring their capacities together, we could reasonably expect better policy and programmatic outcomes and with them a badly needed uptick in public trust in government.

And yet, too often, the well-intended partnerships of center and periphery flounder, unable to reconcile "the juicy, mysterious, ambiguous world of lived experience and organizations' need for abstract documentation for distant audiences" (Eliasoph 2014, 468). The parties find themselves trapped between bureaucratic and community *cultures*, without the translation skills needed to build a bridge. They spar over the *rules* governing the use of grant funds and the documentation of outcomes. They struggle with the proper *scale* for assessing results, since grants typically come as discrete, short-term programs but local networks are interested in improving participant or community-scale indicators over the long haul.

I spent more than two decades interviewing people who worked in positions where they had no choice but to navigate these tensions. The transcripts of those conversations occupy rows of three-ring binders on my bookshelves and dozens of folders and subfolders on my computer. Their pages are filled with the voices of people like Maricela and Hideo: government middle managers, nonprofit executive directors, foundation program officers, employees of faith-related social service organizations, business leaders, program participants, and community residents. I listened closely to the frustrations they experienced in implementing social policy initiatives. I also heard the fresh energy in their voices when they described creative efforts to overcome those frustrations.

It would be easy—and not inaccurate—to hear in the interviews repeated iterations of the tragic story of American poverty and of the drastically diminished public resources devoted to its alleviation. But that is not what the respondents most wanted to talk about. On their mind were the hassles, struggles, and dilemmas of their daily work, experiences that appeared to them as "a series of traps," a phrase memorably evoked by C. Wright Mills (1959, 3) to describe the situation of individuals in modern society. Like Mills, I have come to see the promise of treating these traps—and the ways my respondents coped with those traps—as an opportunity to link "personal troubles of milieu" to "public issues of social structure."

In building this link I focus on a liminal area of governance: the in-between places where people connect the policies, rules, and money flowing from state agencies or private foundations with the local networks and organizations that offer community-based social services. The midlevel managers—public and nonprofit—who work in these spaces must straddle bureaucratic and community cultures and their competing norms: central control versus local discretion; universal rules versus allowance for exceptions; scientific expertise versus local knowledge.

The hidden heroes waste little time debating these abstract ideals or wallowing in their contradictions. Their task is not to explain how the system does or does not work but to make it work for particular people and communities, in situations where uncertainty, ambiguity, and a sense of urgency commingle. Their stories provide a hopefully realistic alternative to the denial or despair that characterizes many recent discussions of democratic prospects.

Resolving Tension to Produce Results

In recent decades, democratic theorists have asserted an understanding of democracy as a productive and results-generating activity.[4] With many democratic processes stifled by gridlock, polarization, or fragmentation, these theorists celebrate exceptions in which results are achieved through problem-focused collaborative governance (Ansell 2011; Ansell and Gash 2008; Boyte and Kari 1996; Briggs 2008; Bryan 2004; Dzur 2008, 2019; Forester 1999; Gardner 2005; Kemmis 1990; Kettl 2006; McIvor 2020; O'Leary et al. 2009; Salamon 2002). While there are many important differences among these voices, they share a preoccupation with overcoming democratic dysfunctions and public disillusionment; with the persistent difficulty we have in "forming a common purpose and carrying it out" (C. Taylor 1991, 112).

A key assumption in this strain of democratic theory is that governance is a process in which people with different mindsets and perspectives have to work together. They meet in ways that reveal the strengths and limits of their respective values and ideals. This coming together creates tension and conflict. At issue is an enduring question: How do these tensions get worked out? The hidden hero stories reveal a fresh way to answer this question. But we first need to consider why their contributions to policy processes are more typically seen as obstacles to be overcome or, alternatively, simply ignored as of little importance.

Consider, for example, the two approaches to public policy that formed the basis of my academic training: one focused on policy implementation, the other on grassroots community organizing. In the former, local administrators were often portrayed as resisting policy directives coming from the federal government, leading to implementation failures. Jeffrey Pressman and Aaron Wildavsky's *Implementation* (1979), a trailblazing study of a job creation program in Oakland, remains the classic treatment. Its unusual subtitle set the tone for a whole genre of similar implementation studies: *How Great Expectations in Washington Are Dashed in Oakland; Or, Why It's Amazing That Federal Programs Work At All, This Being a Saga of the Economic Development Administration, as Told by Two Sympathetic Observers Who Seek to Build Morals on a Foundation of Ruined Hopes.*

Since that time, a common policy analysis storyline has been the *misuse* of local managerial discretion to displace legislatively intended outcomes (Lipsky 1980; Pressman and Wildavsky 1979). Consistent with the traditional understanding of the politics-administration dichotomy (Wilson 1887), many analysts double down on the idea that public managers should work strictly by the book (Hupe and Hill 2006, 18), dutifully following the directives of their superiors in the legislative or executive branches. By contrast, some scholars identify "creative subversion," operating outside the chain of command, as a key skill of innovative public managers (Ban 1995, 13; Levin and Sanger 1994, 217). Herbert Storing (1980, 10) notes that the essence of good administration is the "exercise of experienced, informed, responsible discretion . . . not mere obedience to higher command," adding that this statesmanlike work "tends to be done under cover."

The policy implementation literature identifies a variety of factors driving policy failure, including vague or conflicting policy goals, inadequate provision of resources, a confusing multitude of funding streams with contradictory requirements and rules, lack of provision for local flexibility, local resistance to policy directives, and arbitrary outcome metrics that lead to the "creaming" of clients (Bardach 1977; Christensen 1999; Lipsky 1980; Mazmanian and Sabatier 1989). Commenting on the state of the field in the late 1970s, Pressman and Wildavsky's (1979, 168) droll assessment was that "the capacity of evaluation to detect failure leaped ahead of the ability of implementation to cause success." What they called the "complexity of joint action" is no doubt as difficult today as it was then. Exacerbating the problems is the fragmented U.S. political system, in which "the cards are stacked against things happening, as so much effort is required to make them move" (109).

From Dan Goldrich at the University of Oregon, I learned that the state-community interface was no less challenging when viewed from the perspective of community organizers seeking grassroots-led policy change. From the organizer perspective, public managers and their partners in the nonprofit social services sector serve as defenders of the status quo, more attuned to their bureaucratic superiors or funders than to community voices. But Goldrich also warned students of "the limits of localism"—the difficulty social movements experience in developing forms of expertise capable of exerting influence within complex and technical policy processes:

> Policy that facilitates more public or community control over key decisions paradoxically requires organization on a larger scale. It is now clear that the most fundamental appeal of the community movement, its sense of place and the intimacy of local arenas of action—one of the best expressions of direct democracy—has another highly problematic aspect. It tends to overlook the need to build support across local boundaries for significant policy changes. (Goldrich 1986, 207–208)

In the decades since my graduate training, neoliberal forms of governance have taken center stage. As described by Nikolas Rose (1996, 54–55), one key feature of the neoliberal state is the ascendance of market rationality and with it a privileged place for accounting, evaluation, and monitoring as the types of expertise deemed most relevant to governing. This trend has prompted vigorous debates about the impact of neoliberal managerialism on communities.

In supporting the neoliberal agenda, left and right critics of the welfare state point to the corrupting influence of government funding and tout the innovation and social entrepreneurship possible when the latent power of civil society is freed from bureaucratic shackles (Berger and Neuhaus 1977; Glazer 1988; McKnight 1995). Their opponents counter that the decline in state funding and widespread adoption of market models in delivering social services has compromised the integrity and mission of community-based organizations, who are pressured to abandon or neglect their community roots and social justice functions (Edwards 2010; Eikenberry and Mirabella 2018; Rose 1996). Similar critiques can be found across many different fields of study, including community economic development (DeFilippis 2007); international development (Li 2006); philanthropy (Kohl-Arenas 2015); poverty studies (Hyatt 2001); and food systems (Allen and Guthman 2006).

Amid these debates, the hidden heroes tend to fade from view, as both supporters and critics of the new regime see a stark choice between "state" and "community," with little room for the modulation that might be provided by layers of middle managers. Indeed, one strategy of neoliberal reform is to eliminate those layers, allowing central managers to more directly control what happens at the local level (Sennett 2006). We seem to be trapped within one of two narratives, neither of which considers middle managers as central actors. One describes the destructive colonization of community by hierarchies—bureaucratic, industrial, technological, and others (Berry 1977; Ellul 1964; Habermas 1991; Hyatt 2001; McIvor 2020); the other focuses on the capacity of local people to resist this bureaucratic inundation (Kohl-Arenas 2015; Scott 1990, 1998; Wells 1996).

It is hard to understand the hidden heroes within either the state-centric or community-empowerment models of policy change. They occupy positions that straddle vertical and horizontal loyalties and commitments. Faced with the clash of cultures, they move the governance process forward by embracing tension in creative ways. Overall, their examples point toward a different and more balanced perspective on power and policy, one that is honest about the strengths and limitations of both state bureaucracies and community-based organizations and cognizant of their need for one another.

Set against the intellectual horizon painted by the prevailing theories of policy and power, the stories told by the hidden heroes stand as anomalies, exhibiting a subtlety and complexity missing in the sometimes-shrill academic debates. They have prompted me to consider questions that have been overlooked by most scholars: How might the strengths of bureaucracy be deployed in ways that support the autonomy of local groups, coalitions, or collaboratives? And vice versa: How might organized citizens and communities enable the programs bureaucracy deploys to better align with the interests of local publics? Finally, what capacities and practices enable the hidden heroes to facilitate this alignment, in the face of deeply rooted governance tensions and contradictions?

How the Hidden Hero Stories Were Gathered

So far we have identified (1) a liminal space in our governance where two necessary but not easily combined ways of understanding and acting on the world meet, (2) a set of people whose work requires them to navigate the tensions and conflicts that characterize that space, and (3) a fresh set of questions to ask about what leads to successful policy implementation. In this section, I describe how research teams I led gathered the case examples that support my contention that these spaces, people, and questions deserve a more central place in our study of public policy.[5]

The research began in simple curiosity. I wondered how new governance reforms—devolution, integrated services, results accountability—were playing out in local communities. The reformers sought to create effective, results-oriented partnerships between central funders and local grantees. During the same period, community organizing networks began to reject the view that bureaucratic institutions are always the enemy. Both shifts held out the promise of improving public policy and the delivery of public services. I saw the promise but also the need to document what was actually happening as the reform ideas hit the ground. That documentation—in the form of applied research and evaluation projects conducted in local communities—eventually took me to every corner of the socially and geographically diverse state of California.

The governance reforms were hitting their stride just as I was beginning an academic career at the University of California, Davis, in the early 1990s. As a Cooperative Extension Specialist, my role was to conduct community studies that illuminated and informed trends in governance, economic development, and leadership. The community engagement arm of land grant universities, Cooperative Extension embodies two distinct purposes. On the one hand, it produces and disseminates expert knowledge and technology to spur economic progress. On the other hand, it develops community capacity to devise locally specific solutions to problems that they themselves define (Peters 2010). At its best, the organization finds creative ways to honor both scientific expertise and local voice, knitting together their respective strengths. At its worst, the organization falls prey to the tendency to pit these ideals against each other, taking sides in ways that become part of the problem. Being aware of the opportunities and struggles within Cooperative Extension alerted me to similar tensions in the organizations I was studying.

Early in my career I began receiving requests to evaluate collaborative community initiatives of many types. These included government welfare and workforce development programs and private foundation initiatives supporting child development, youth civic engagement, and healthy communities. Though their substantive focus varied, the projects shared a common hope and a related stricture. The hope was to revitalize civil society by engaging communities more actively in the work of governance, making them less reliant on government itself. In return, government and private foundation funders wanted local partners to tell them not just what they were doing with grant resources but what outcomes of public value resulted. The initiatives imagined tapping the power of local civil society and social capital but within funding parameters and accountability requirements controlled by central bureaucracies, either public or private. The tension between those two aspirations became the thread or storyline that connected all the applied research I conducted.

My fieldwork, conducted over a span of three decades from the mid-1990s to 2021, engaged me with governance reform experiments in three different roles: as an extension educator training others in outcomes assessment principles and techniques, as an observer of funder-grantee relationships, and as an evaluator charged myself with documenting the results of collaborative community initiatives. My field of study became the evolving relationships linking government and foundations to various governmental, nonprofit, and private entities in local communities.

Research teams I led or co-led conducted applied research in diverse urban, rural, and suburban settings. Data we collected included more than 2,000 interviews as well as hundreds of meeting observations, comparative analysis of census and administrative data, and the collection of informal background information from Cooperative Extension colleagues who lived in the communities where projects were taking place.

The projects included eight major evaluations leading to formal reports.[6] All eight included results accountability requirements. In some cases, such as government-funded workforce development programs, success metrics were clearly and precisely specified, and future funding was directly tied to meeting performance targets. In others, including the foundation-funded civic engagement initiatives, expected outcomes were less rigidly defined, yet a results mindset still loomed large, embedded in program logic models, grantee reporting requirements, and evaluation objectives. Over time, it became possible to view the eight projects as natural experiments in how well results accountability processes were working in actual, ground-level experience.

While we had many opportunities to directly observe the projects, our research primarily relied on interviews with local actors, whose context-laden narratives give particularity, contingency, ambiguity, and flux their due measure. The analyst who earns the trust of local informants can gain access to "hidden transcripts" (Scott 1990) that express thoughts respondents are reluctant to share directly with their funders or bureaucratic superiors. They talk about failures, unmet challenges, persistent trade-offs, and frustration with funder rules and requirements. They also talk about successes that came about by breaking the rules (Campbell 2012). At the same time, our work was informed by the perspectives of funders, whose goals and priorities shaped our evaluation designs and with whom we interacted in both formal interviews and informal reporting relationships. By accessing both the local and central authority perspectives and holding these in tension with each other, we were able to bring into view challenges and possibilities that neither perspective by itself could make available. Our research and evaluation teams dutifully tracked metrics of success, based on project goals. But we also sought to answer the question of why the results, intended or unintended, had occurred or failed to occur. The "Why?" question led us into a world marked by practical judgment, local knowledge, improvisational experimentation, iterative conversation, and rooted-in-context leadership. In our evaluation reports—normally narrowly focused on whether local implementers use resources prudently and achieve what was intended—we increasingly felt compelled to talk back to funders. We asked them to consider how their standard ways of doing business were hamstringing local implementation, undercutting the funders' own goals, and disrupting the community development processes that preceded the grant. Grantees needed reminders as well. They often alternated between wanting funders to support the "good work" they do, without much regard for results, and the opposite extreme of embracing a too rigid and unrealistic view of what would constitute a scientifically valid set of outcome measures. In these and other ways, we found funder-grantee relationships to be sites of persistent tension. Too often their relationship, built on the pursuit of shared civic goals, degenerated into feelings of confusion or resentment.

I would be remiss if I did not also report, in this initial overview, two more encouraging findings. First, despite challenges in how results accountability was practiced, we observed significant outcomes of public value in every project. These results sometimes mirrored the preset objectives of government or foundation funders. But they often included valued outcomes not anticipated in those grants or linked to a planned program. I grew to appreciate the unheralded, everyday heroes who made these results possible. They managed to reframe, in practical and actionable terms, conflicts that appear irresolvable when expressed as academic abstractions.

These hidden heroes implement funded programs, but they do so within a set of broader commitments and concerns, including protecting staff time, supporting community partners, recognizing the individual circumstances of program participants, and maintaining the effective functioning of key community institutions: schools, workforce programs, social service departments, public health agencies, and nonprofit organizations, among others. We take for granted the existence of these community institutions but too often fail to attend to their health and vitality, which is essential to achieving public purposes. The hidden heroes do not have that luxury.

Second, in spaces where the participants were discussing and reflecting on matters of public concern—public meetings, interviews, and such—they often experienced animation, fun, and even joy. This was true not in spite of the challenges they faced but because of the satisfactions they found in crafting effective responses together. As we see in later chapters, there is something laudable and instructive about the *way* the hidden heroes cope with the governance tensions where bureaucracy meets community, with *how* they do it. Meeting difficulty as they do enlarges their sense of competence. They gain the ability to say, with conviction, "We did it, and our doing it made a difference."

This is no trivial matter. The most fundamental need of human beings is for a sense of effective agency (Bettelheim 1967; Seligman 1975). It is a kind of competence in context that is called forth when we take seriously our obligation to excellence in policy implementation, an ability to stay true to our intentions in the midst of the resistances we encounter. In a culture that typically views public life as a drain on emotional energies (Sennett 1974), we tend to dismiss the pleasures and sense of accomplishment public work can bring. If there is a way forward for our democracy, it will require that more of us experience these delights of public life.

Recap and Preview

This book digs deep into the question of how policy results are achieved, but without attaching itself to one or another of the prevailing theories about how this best occurs. Instead, I burrow into the places where results often go to die, to the in-between spaces where bureaucratic hierarchies and networks of community organizations intersect. Here we find individuals whose everyday work straddles bureaucratic and community worlds. The competing ideals of these worlds pull in opposing and seemingly contradictory directions. Yet the two need to come together if policies and programs are to succeed. We will be examining how this happens in the routine work of the hidden heroes of our democracy. Paying attention to the hidden heroes answers the call by Pierre and Peters (2021, 118) to insert agency into the study of governance, avoiding the "danger that governance theory is written in the passive voice without identifying the actors who are important for moving the governance process forward."

There are several competing ideals that create tension in contemporary governance, many of which come into play in the case examples I share. Among these, I have chosen to put special analytic emphasis on two essential—and essentially incompatible—forms of usable knowledge: metrics and mētis. To understand the hidden hero narratives, it is necessary to appreciate the clash between these disparate ways of knowing and acting on the world.

In making this choice of emphasis, I want to acknowledge two particularly important intellectual debts. While my training and professional experiences set the stage, it was reading James Scott's *Seeing Like a State* (1998) that provided the spark animating this book. Scott offers a festival of examples showing the dependence of formal bureaucratic order on informal community processes "which the formal scheme does not recognize, without which it could not exist, and which it alone cannot create or maintain" (Scott 1998, 310–311). In invoking the Greek word "mētis" (Detienne and Vernant 1978) to describe the practical wisdom those informal processes embody, Scott planted the seed that alerted me to the interplay of metrics and mētis in routine grantmaking practices.

At about the same time, I was introduced to Peter Elbow's *Embracing Contraries* (1986), explorations in learning and teaching from a professor of English. Elbow believes that wisdom has a characteristically dialectical shape. His exemplar is not Hegel but Chaucer. The former brought us the famous thesis-antithesis-synthesis pattern in which contradictory elements are transcended at a higher level. According to Elbow, Chaucer's dialectic is more subtle: "By setting up a polar opposition and affirming both sides, he lays the groundwork for a larger frame of reference. . . . He arranges the dilemma so that we can only be satisfied by taking a larger view" (1986, 240). If this book succeeds, those who study policy or are engaged in policy implementation will have a better idea what that larger view entails.

The remainder of the book is organized as follows. Chapter 2 explores the contrast between metrics and mētis, the history of previous attempts to reconcile their contradictions, and the ways they interacted in the programmatic and geographic contexts in which my encounter with the hidden heroes took place.

Chapters 3 through 5 form the core of the book, taking up stories of how the hidden heroes reframe abstractly cast governance dilemmas in practical and actionable terms. Chapter 3 takes up the collision of bureaucratic and community cultures. Chapter 4 examines conflicts over the rules and compliance demands that accompany grants, including rules about outcome reporting. Chapter 5 examines difficulties in determining the proper scale for assessing outcomes, calling into question the exclusive reliance on program-centric evaluation. In all three of these empirically based chapters, I pursue a balanced approach, blending a realistic portrayal of challenges with evidence of how these can spark effective expressions of democratic agency. The focus is on illustrating the everyday accommodations and craft practices that the hidden heroes deploy: developing workarounds, sidestepping rules, shifting the unit of analysis from programs to networks, and practicing cultural humility, among others.

Chapter 6 and 7 draw on the evidence to consider implications for theory, policy, and practice. Chapter 6 focuses on what the hidden heroes teach us about the nature of evaluative assessment, which is ubiquitous not only in the policy worlds this book examines but throughout our everyday lives. I ask: How can assessment be conducted in ways that are fair to the people and programs being evaluated? How can funder reporting requirements and other rituals of evaluation enhance rather than detract from the pursuit of intended outcomes? How might both funders and local implementers put their best foot forward, not to evade accountability but to allow it to spur continuous learning and improved outcomes?

Chapter 7 highlights the role of hidden hero leadership in creating the policy results we intend. I highlight both the concrete leadership practices the hidden heroes deploy and the distinctive frame of reference they bring to their work—an ability to hold tension and embrace contraries. The larger point of view and the specific practices work hand in hand to create possibilities where others perceive only road-blocks.

The deeper I dug into the dilemmas facing the hidden heroes, the more I realized they are not dissimilar from those confronting all of us in the places where we live and work. In these everyday settings, we encounter the characteristic pinch of modern life, between our dependence on bureaucratic resources and expertise and the equally compelling need to honor the particularities of people and place. This tension provides an ongoing curriculum in the arts of democratic practice, calling forth an everyday heroism at once purposeful, activating, and broadly available.

2

Governing Where Metrics Meet Mētis

Of the hundreds of field interviews I have conducted, one in particular haunts me. It took place in a living room in Los Banos, California. My colleague Joan Wright and I were there to get a single mother's perspective on the Merced County Attendance Project (MerCAP), which the state Department of Social Services had hired our University of California, Davis, team to evaluate.

The project was the brainchild of a member of the county's Board of Supervisors, a response to one of the less heralded provisions in the 1996 welfare reform legislation. That provision listed good school attendance as a condition of receiving welfare cash assistance. Merced was the first county in California to launch a formal welfare school attendance program, under a waiver from the state allowing our research team to compare the attendance data of students whose families received cash assistance with those who did not (Campbell and Wright 2005). The program covered children ages six to fifteen. Failure to meet the attendance requirement resulted in a fiscal sanction that reduced the family's cash assistance by the amount for that child for a minimum of one month. The intention was that early intervention would reduce absenteeism rates that are linked to low school achievement, school dropouts, poor preparation for work, and related problems in later years.

As we spoke to the mom, her nine-year-old son and six-year-old daughter sat listening. From the vantage point of standard program metrics, the family was a welfare reform success story: the mom had recently found a job, and the two children were attending school regularly. But if you looked beyond those metrics, a more disturbing picture came into view. The mother's job was in San Jose. To get to work on time, she had to leave every morning at 5:30 A.M. for the long and uncertain commute "over the hill," as the locals refer to it. Her pay was so meager that she and her children still qualified for welfare payments. Those payments were subject to county sanction if her children accrued more than ten unexcused absences during the school year.

The young boy, a third grader, was now responsible for getting not only himself up, fed, and off to school but his younger sister as well. As we spoke to his mom, and then briefly with him, the boy's anxiety was palpable. He worried that he would screw up and cost the family precious dollars. Our presence as evaluators heightened his angst: people were watching, judging. A program whose basic assumption was that his mother was likely to act irresponsibly if not subject to sanction was landing on the slight shoulders of a young boy eager to do the right thing.

Joan and I faced an evaluative conundrum: how, if at all, to reconcile the metrics indicating success with the deeply troubling living room perspective. The metrics would eventually travel across scales, communicating information that central decision-makers considered important. Whether or not the young boy's experience could make a similar journey was less certain. Both were evidence-based results of the project, but their implications for program accountability ran in very different directions.

The Troubled Marriage of Metrics and Mētis

At the nexus where center and periphery uneasily meet, we encounter a governance dilemma posed by two essential—and essentially incompatible—forms of knowledge: metrics and mētis. The former is a ubiquitous tool for simplifying the exchange of information, commonly used by central authorities to monitor and control their distant peripheries (Porter 1995). The latter is an ancient word for practical wisdom or cunning, a type of knowledge that grows from devoted attention to the particularities of place and personal circumstance (Detienne and Vernant 1978; Scott 1998).[1]

Over recent decades, proponents of new governance reforms such as devolution and integrated services saw the promise of combining these two ideas using an approach called results accountability. The core logic can be simply stated: funders specify the outcomes being sought and hold program implementers accountable via standardized metrics while giving implementers flexibility to use context-sensitive judgment to decide *how* they achieve the outcomes in particular settings.

Viewed in the abstract, results accountability appears to solve a vexing problem facing the reformers. Because devolution and integrated services reforms rely on extended networks of government, nonprofit, and private organizations to run programs, they "vest substantial discretionary authority in entities other than those with ultimate responsibility for results," such that "government agencies are no longer in control of the programs they administer" (Salamon 2002, 603). At the same time, the public holds the government responsible when these programs fail to deliver what they promise. The reformers hoped that requiring evidence of measurable outcomes would address the accountability challenges both internally and externally. Results accountability would provide "a disciplined way of thinking and taking action" (Friedman 2005, 11), help government managers regain a measure of control over local networks, free program implementers from red tape, and focus resources on proven programs to satisfy a cost-averse public (Friedman 2005; Gardner 1995; Gore 1993; Schorr 1989).

It is an appealing promise: to reconcile the respective democratic claims of center and periphery, those with resources and those in communities that those resources are intended to serve. Ideally this reconciliation would respect and enhance the autonomy and commitments of each party. In establishing intended results to which resources are being devoted, government funders are responding—however imperfectly—to the legitimate expressions of public will as expressed through elections, legislative processes, or executive authority. In making sure that resources are deployed in ways that honor unique local circumstances, or the reasonable claims of particular individuals, local implementers are translating preconceived program designs to ensure responsiveness to the particular publics and communities they serve. In these two very different ways, metrics and mētis each contribute to democratic legitimacy and the achievement of collective civic purposes.

Yet the marriage of metrics and mētis is a troubled one. Held too tightly or exclusively, each of these ways of knowing and ordering the public world undermines what is valuable in the other. Mētis-laden policy adjustments are suffocated if overly constrained by rule-bound procedures or preset performance targets. Likewise, metrics lose their ability to serve as an objective point of reference if taken out of context or used cunningly to advance a particular interest or agenda. Rather than combining seamlessly to enhance democracy and realize policy objectives, as the reformers intend, the juxtaposition of metrics and mētis generates conflict that can short-circuit well-intended efforts to improve community well-being and the lives of disadvantaged citizens.

Leaning on these disparate forms of knowledge, the rhetorical reach of results accountability typically exceeds its practical grasp. This might cause concern but should not surprise us. As one observer notes, "What appears to be rational from the reformer's lofty perch is frequently irrational from the worm's eye perspective of those charged with implementing the reforms" (Harmon 1995, 3).

Comparing the Role and Nature of Metrics and Mētis

Theodore Porter (1995) makes a convincing case that the privileged position of metrics in contemporary life is born not of bureaucratic power but of institutional vulnerability and weakness. Skepticism of institutions and experts flourishes, and official judgments are often challenged. Numbers precisely arrived at provide a defense, a way for decision-makers to appear fair and impartial. By appearing to exclude judgment and individual discretion, metrics support expert decisions, universal rules, compliance demands, or best-practice recommendations.

The embrace of quantification becomes a way to claim neutrality while exercising authority across large scales, without the trust and local knowledge made possible in communities bound by culture, sentiment, personal relationships, and face-to-face dialogue. Metrics are a "technology of distance" (Porter 1995, ix), a means of communicating information in standardized forms, necessary to enforce fiscal or programmatic accountability within extended service delivery networks. Rose (1996) makes a similar point, noting that expertise becomes the way that the liberal state reconciles the reality of limited government with the need to exercise rule across time and space, "to govern at a distance" (43).

The essence of mētis, by contrast, is "plastic, local, and divergent" (Scott 1998, 332). Exercising mētis requires a knack or feel for what is going on and an ability to adapt to concrete and constantly evolving situations. Working with mētis engages the powers of human empathy and the crafts of competent action, rather than the ready-made scripts of doctrine, technique, program, or best practice. Mētis thrives in a world of highly subjective judgment and discretion. On the periphery or bottom rungs of hierarchies, it provides a cunning way for the less powerful to modulate, outwit, or evade the reach of central authorities. But since every place is local to its denizens, there are also forms of mētis that operate within all the many layers of a bureaucracy.

Scott (1998) makes three assertions that have shaped my own approach to understanding the interplay of metrics and mētis in governance: (1) mētis includes cunning intelligence rooted in experience but also encompasses a wide range of everyday skills necessary to produce practical results (313); (2) mētis is a form of knowledge embedded in local, particular contexts in contrast to the technical knowledge employed by the state and bureaucratic agencies who must manage at a distance (311); and, importantly, (3) a working collaboration between the two forms of knowledge is needed but often difficult, underappreciated, or hidden (310).

Within what might appear on the surface to be highly rational results accountability processes, metrics and mētis find themselves enmeshed in complex ways. It turns out that every metric is built on mētis-laden practical judgments and trade-offs (e.g., validity vs. feasibility/cost), while every exercise of mētis presumes, at some level, a goal beyond the immediate situation that might lend itself to an indicator metric. Seemingly objective numbers often prove less "hard" on closer inspection of data collection processes, which can be lax or manipulated with particular ends in mind. While we might hope that metrics become tools of value-neutral learning, numbers often become ammunition for political combat or bureaucratic reprisal. They can be used by the powerful against the politically weak or by the weak to convey an emotionally urgent need for action: "This cannot stand."

We rely on metrics so that judgment can be decisive and unassailable, but the reality they depict is often complex. While quantified metrics are built to travel readily across scales, their meanings do so imperfectly, as context-sensitive interpretation gives way to simplistic or misleading explanations. As Shapin (2010, 340) puts it: "Fixed, quantitative and seemingly reliable knowledge loses its power when it is stripped of its oral, situated, and purposive setting. The same knowledge expressed as a general rule becomes nonsense, but when expressed in the particular context of practical use makes sense."

Our brains find anecdotes and stories more memorable than statistics because they are more emotionally engaging (James et al. 2020). This may not always be the problem some make it out to be. Because stories can convey nuance and capture ambiguity, they sometimes give us a better handle on experience. Ideally, metrics and mētis-infused storytelling are mutually enriching and reinforcing, but this is not always how we use them.

The implications of these insights into the relationship of metrics and mētis have yet to adequately inform our thinking about democratic governance and policy implementation, in part because theorists tend to take sides in advancing their cases. From one direction we learn of *The Tyranny of Metrics* (Muller 2018) and *Limits of the Numerical* (Newfield, Alexandrova, and John 2022); from the other we are advised to pursue *Evidence-Based Policy* (Cartwright and Hardie 2012; see also Singer 2015) and to be *Measuring Program Outcomes* (United Way 1996). There are important truths in all these perspectives, but it is rare to find a synthesis that honors their respective insights.

Balancing Metrics and Mētis for Policy Success

I have come to the conclusion that the reformers were correct in asserting that we need both metrics and mētis. As different as they are from each other, we must find effective ways to marry these disparate forms of knowledge if our public policy and community development processes are to meet the twin tests of democratic legitimacy and programmatic effectiveness. Commenting on a rare set of successful social service reforms, Lisbeth Schorr (1997, 113) notes: "In each of these examples, public officials and administrators have recognized the distinction between the functions that must be standardized from the top down and those whose effectiveness hinges on being responsive to specific individuals, families, and communities."

The same call for balance is found in a recent review of the implementation of evidence-based practices by federal agencies: "Federal funding agencies (as well as other funders) face competing goals. On the one hand, funders can play a positive role in promoting more and better use of evidence toward more effective and efficient programming. On the other hand, grantmaking is an opportunity to foster innovation and community-specific adaptation in the provision of services. Pursuing either goal exclusively could undermine the other" (Horne et al. 2021, 251).

At issue is *how* to forge this balance. The practical challenge facing democracy's hidden heroes is inextricably tied to the conceptual task of reintegrating "what the modern world and its theories of knowledge have split apart" (Boyte 2021, 13). On one side of the divide are the forces of centralization, technology, scientific expertise, bureaucracy, complex organizations, secularism, professional specialization, quantification, formal procedures, rational-comprehensive planning, and rules as determiners of action. On the other side are decentralization, craftsmanship, local knowledge, adaptive management, community control, voluntary and faith-related organizations, citizen engagement and self-help, face-to-face social bonds and trust, informal processes, and folkways.

Shaped by these contraries, we have come to assume that bureaucracies and community networks are, in most important respects, antithetical. Listening to the stories of the hidden heroes leads me to wonder if—in drawing the distinctions so tightly and abstractly—we are denying ourselves the possibility of a more useful and animating public story. What if our story is not simply the triumph of bureaucracy at the expense of community, or their ongoing estrangement? What if we construe our story, and the problem of democratic agency in our time, as their ongoing struggle to achieve a form of collective competence that neither by itself can realize?

Realizing this vision is inherently challenging in a society of complex organizations, where bureaucracy distances those at the top from the base, leading to dysfunctions and resentments of many kinds. Neither bureaucrat bashing or romantic notions of community empowerment will suffice; we need democratic practices that wed the best aspects of detached expertise and universal standards with the craft of adaptive local management offering "fit to place."[2]

An Enduring Dilemma

It is a dilemma that first vexed public administration a century ago and continues to bewilder today: how to wed central control and expertise with appropriate measures of local discretion and citizen participation. As historian Robert Wiebe (1995, 211) wryly observes, "How to combine the two was not self-evident," then or now.

Early work in public administration was acutely aware of the dilemma, treating it as a tension to be artfully traversed. Three quick examples should suffice to make the point. When Mary Parker Follett (1926) penned her essay on the giving and taking of orders, her purpose was to render problematic this taken-for-granted transaction. She realized that unless the communication was conducted with care, it would undermine the self-respect of the subordinate, leading to declining morale, diminished sense of responsibility, and efforts to sabotage orders. Her solution was that superiors and subordinates needed to view themselves as jointly facing "the situation at hand," coming to a shared understanding of what should be done and acknowledging mutual responsibility for the results. In her rendering, "the situation at hand" provides the disciplining force on action, rather than the discipline being located solely in abstract orders or rules.

Likewise, when David Lilienthal (1944) wrote about planning in the Tennessee Valley, he went out of his way to argue that implementation strategies could not be divorced from what the people of the region could be persuaded to commit to in the course of their daily lives. Planning required the democratic mobilization of common purpose to succeed. The process was necessarily incremental and iterative, as expert ideas were adapted to local realities. Faced with criticism that this approach was too slow and subverted what expert planners recommended, Lilienthal insisted that was a reasonable price to pay since the alternative was coercion that would rob the people of their democratic freedoms. Patient efforts to educate the public were the alternative to allowing experts to simply take over.

A third example comes from Camilla Stivers's (2000) history showing how the men leading the early development of public administration sought legitimacy by claiming the mantle of business-like efficiency, undergirded by newly developed quantitative methods and social statistics. Their embrace of scientific management and metrics was challenged by women in the settlement house movement, whose version of science emphasized immersion in the experiments of daily life rather than the abstractions of statistical data. These women were already experiencing what many bemoan today: human beings being treated as cases because of the deployment of standardized programs. At issue was whether a version of governance dependent on the passion for self-government nurtured in neighborhoods and communities could survive as government bureaucracy grew in scope.

While there is broad agreement that the Progressive era marked a key historical turning point in which these questions of democratic governance became urgent, the meaning of the societal changes continues to be debated. For political scientist Robert Putnam, the early 1900s era began an "upswing" evident throughout the first two-thirds of the twentieth century, as evidenced by "steady upward progress toward *greater* economic equality, *more* cooperation in the public sphere, a *stronger* social fabric, and a *growing* culture of solidarity" (2020, 10, emphasis in the original). Recalling Alexis de Tocqueville's observation of the American penchant for civic association, his account links grassroots civic associations and government experts as part of a broader "we" committed to civic improvement, thus overcoming the Gilded Age's overemphasis on individual liberty.

Other accounts paint a darker picture, emphasizing how the ascendance of experts undermined the culture of democratic self-rule. Historian Wiebe (1995) documents the early twentieth-century shift from a communitarian form of democracy to one that assumed hierarchy and inequality, justified by differences in education and status. Henceforth, experts would solve problems on behalf of a deactivated citizenry. Meeting people's needs effectively and efficiently became the state's role, with or (increasingly) without popular participation. Tocqueville is cited for a different purpose in this account. He famously feared democratic despotism, in which sovereign power "does not tyrannize" but through "a network of small, complicated rules, minute and uniform . . . compresses, enervates, extinguishes, and stupefies a people, till each nation is reduced to be nothing better than a flock of timid and industrious animals" (Tocqueville 1945, 337).

Those fears proved eerily prophetic when a mechanical engineer turned management consultant seemingly took Tocqueville's metaphor literally, arguing that the ideal steelworker should "be so stupid and so phlegmatic that he more nearly resembles in his mental makeup the ox" (F. Taylor 1911, 59). The deskilling of workers envisioned by Fredrick Taylor enshrined managerial control in the workplace (Braverman 1974). Less obviously but equally consequentially, the political theory of progressivism enshrined it in the polity, placing the burden of solving public problems on professionally trained civil servants deploying quantifiable metrics rather than civic-minded citizens displaying practical judgment and mētis-laden improvisation (Kemmis 1990; Schwartz and Sharpe 2010; Wiebe 1995). Danger lurked on this path: the reliance of government on scientific knowledge could turn the public into a "helpless, unthinking followership" (Stivers 2000, 81).

Wiebe's history reminds us that the logic of devolution we sometimes think of as a recent trend had many antecedents. The emerging progressive regime attempted to hold center and periphery together by means of an uneasy truce between national and local elites, in which the former would set national economic policy while the latter would get a portion of the center's resources and some freedom to set the rules in their own locations, along with accountability for the results (Wiebe 1995). Over time this arrangement shifted, as national social policies increasingly set the terms of what rights and benefits the poor could expect, while local government implemented policies set on high.

Immerwahr's (2015) history of community development picks up the story from there, showing how the proponents of centralization and modernization never fully succeeded in keeping communitarian alternatives at bay. Regular debates in foreign and domestic policy pitted expert-designed, top-down strategies against local knowledge and citizen engagement. The War on Poverty strategy of "maximum feasible participation" of the poor during the Johnson administration is a prominent example. Landing amid urban unrest and a nascent social revolution, the strategy empowered community-based organizations that sought changes that many elites deemed too radical. Federal officials eventually backed off the more participatory elements of poverty programs, handing control of federal resources back to local elites.

With national funding came national rules. Donald Kettl's (1980) analysis of the community development block grant program of the 1970s documents "creeping categorization" whereby local elite discretion gradually gave way to tighter administrative controls imposed by federal bureaucrats. The strictures came with multiple justifications: evidence that some locals misused federal funds; the inability of local administrators to effectively manage programs given their limited resources and expertise; and political pressure from interest groups who argued the funds were not helping the poor as intended. As Gardner (2005) notes, the shift in emphasis from centralization to devolution and back are part of the ongoing negotiations between cities and counties and their state and federal funders. Results accountability is part of any deal that grants local agencies more discretion.

The Same Dilemma "Viewed from Below"

For those who assume that democracy requires active citizenship to flourish, the problem is how to promote this within or outside bureaucratic structures whose tendency is to marginalize public voices. With typical vividness, David Matthews (2014, 58) captures the semantic root of the difficulty: "Citizens are more likely to tell a *personal* story when they name a problem than they are to issue a statistical report: the language of professional culture is primarily metric, but the language of civic life is not."

Over time, scholars working in this tradition have defined the obstacles in a variety of ways depending on the civic engagement strategy they favor. Each of these adds something important to our understanding of the problem; none of them resolve it.

Citizen Participation

This term incorporates a wide range of actual practices. As categorized in Sherry Arnstein's (1969) iconic "ladder of citizen participation," there are eight levels from "manipulation" to "citizen control." Federal, state, and local public agencies have a long history of engaging the public to provide input to shape policy formation, implementation, or evaluation. Proponents tout the benefits of these approaches in bringing about more responsive public policies. Critics emphasize the tendency of these elite-managed processes to foster co-optation: citizens are provided occasions to vent their grievances, but bureaucrats still run the day-to-day details of policy. Even the more organized and effective change agents can be co-opted "through programs that bring protest leaders into the 'system'" (Dye and Zeigler 1987, 413) or by elites who embrace their issues but in a superficial way (Buttel 1992, 13). As Kenneth Dolbeare and Murray Edelman (1985, 508) put it, "When the process has run its course, some new policies have been instituted, the basic complaints against the system have been reduced, the establishment has absorbed new members, and the system has acquired new defenders. The basic outlines of the system have again survived."

From this perspective, democratic initiatives that honor citizen voice will at some point have to come to grips with what bureaucrats and elite power holders are willing to entertain. Further, local citizens will need to learn to communicate in the metric-infused terms those power holders take for granted.

Community Organizing

The community organizing tradition takes entrenched power seriously from the start. In the Saul Alinsky tradition, the twin enemies are giant corporations with their concentrations of wealth and power and the modern state bureaucracy, acting in concert with corporations and exercising its own forms of unchecked authority (M. Miller 1978). The solution is to counter this power by building independent, broad-based people's organizations that can identify winnable issues and pressure elected officials using electoral involvement, demonstrations, or more disruptive tactics.

Many others have recounted the variety of forms this vibrant tradition has taken and its record of success and failure in supporting policy change (Alinsky 1961; Boyte 1989; Horwitt 1989; Pierce 1984; Warren 2001). Sustaining these citizens' organizations has been a particular challenge, leading the community organizing movement to begin rooting their work in existing institutions like local churches or labor unions. This institutional turn put community organizations and their leaders in a better position to link their initiatives with bureaucratic resources, as we explore in Chapter 3.

Deliberative Democracy

Deliberative democracy is still another approach to elevating public voices. A variety of techniques have been used, such as issue forums (Matthews and McAfee 2003), deliberative polls (Fishkin 1991), citizen juries (Crosby, Kelley, and Schaefer 1986), representative survey panels (Weeks 2000), participatory budgets (Baiocchi 2001), and a deliberation day during every presidential election year (Ackerman and Fishkin 2004).

By shifting the terrain on which citizens and bureaucratic officials meet, deliberative democrats attempt to sidestep the danger of cooptation or the difficulties of broad-scale community organizing. They do so by creating independent forums they control, with the goal of equalizing power imbalances. In the version of this work with which I am most familiar—the Kettering Foundation public issue forum model (Matthews and McAfee 2003)—all participants are asked to "take their hats off at the door," adopting an open-minded and presumably less biased approach to whatever policy issue is being debated. If only it were that simple. Drawing on the work of Jurgen Habermas (1991), David McIvor (2020) provides a helpful counterpoint. Those promoting deliberation within a model of collaborative governance cannot escape the structural tensions and political power relationships that are the context for the conversation.

For Caroline Lee (2007, 91), the preoccupation in this field with formal models and techniques slights the important role informal communication plays in deliberative processes and threatens to turn "participation" into another expert-dominated industry. Tanya Murray Li (2006, 34) puts the operative thinking in even blunter terms, bemoaning a "governmental stance that envisioned empowerment as a product that could be manufactured by technique." Armed with a toolbox of preferred techniques, experts descend into communities in ways that too often repeat the mistakes of the bureaucrats they hope to supplant (Lee 2007, 91). Rosemary McGee (2002, 107) laments a "blindness to context, leading to mechanistic applications of participatory techniques." Noting that "the success or failure of deliberation depends so much on its context," Dennis Thompson (2008, 511) identifies inherent trade-offs and tensions within the work: "We miss the complexity and power of deliberative democracy if we do not recognize the possibility that its elements may conflict with one another, that not all the goods it promises can be secured at the same time, and that we have to make choices among them."

Public Work

With its emphasis on action-oriented public work among diverse individuals, the field of civic studies offers an alternative to approaches emphasizing talk alone. A key obstacle is "identity-based exclusion," the difficulty of recognizing the "we" that can act together in a world intent on defining itself as "us" and "them."[3] We are familiar with how this infects our politics along left-right ideological dimensions. But it is increasingly obvious that this problem is interrelated with vertically defined "us-them" tensions separating bureaucratic experts from members of the public.

Elinor Ostrom (2002, 2010) and Harry Boyte (2004) provide coherent frameworks that articulate ways to overcome this problem of identity-based exclusion. At the heart of Ostrom's work is the principle of "fitting institutional rules to a specific social-ecological setting" (2010, 642). Community members are not hopelessly trapped by the structure of the situation but can exercise self-reflection and creativity. She emphasizes the importance of ongoing learning, consistent with the idea of mētis-infused adaptation. Boyte and Nancy Kari remind us that "effective citizenship thus depends on people thinking of themselves as productive: people who can build things and do things, people who come up with ideas and resources; people who are

bold; people who are accountable" (1996, 24). The public work tradition
these scholars advance has an answer to situations where clear indicator metrics are hard to come by: "look at what we built together."

Governance in the Post–Welfare Reform Era

My encounter with the hidden heroes took place during the era that
followed federal welfare reform legislation. The fieldwork began with
a study of how California counties were implementing the new welfare policies. The changes embodied in that legislation came to mark
a new phase in American social policy but grew out of broader cur-
rents in the economy and culture.

During recent decades, as consumer goods grew cheaper and
working-class jobs disappeared, the relatively high costs of govern-
ment-provided human services received increasing scrutiny from
politicians and the public (Muller 2018, 44). Turning the Progressive
era assumption on its head, bureaucrats became viewed by many as
the problem (Zacka 2017). Neoliberal regimes looked to the market
and voluntary sectors to play a greater role in community governance, sparking administrative reform under the banner of the new
public management.

Increasingly, the federal role became defined by its audit and compliance functions rather than by its direction of redistributive policies. The social policy world became defined by short-term, piece-
meal projects, often administered through outcome-based contracts
with nongovernmental entities or taking shape within small-scale
community self-help projects. Traditional public administration had
to adapt to a new world of network governance, which provided a less
clear-cut set of targets around which community organizers might
rally neighborhood residents to action.

The new public management was seen as a way to avoid expanding the number of public employees and to evade the rule-bound rigidity of traditional public administration. It has broadened frontline
discretion in ways both helpful and highly problematic (Brodkin and
Marston 2013; Kettl 2015; Soss, Fording, and Schram 2011). Importantly, even where this approach partially succeeds in mediating metric-
mētis tensions, it reduces the government's capacity to create results
of sufficient scope to justify increased public investment. Whether de-

liberately or as an unintended effect, this dynamic has contributed to long-term disinvestment in social programs. It also has given rise to the growing (but not entirely new) demand for results accountability as a way to monitor and improve social programs or, alternatively, justify reductions in or outright elimination of their funding. Still, the larger goals of new governance reformers contained significant promise. Devolution was seen as a way to reinvigorate local civil society, including both local governments whose power and influence had been waning for decades (Sokolow and Detwiler 2001) and nonprofit organizations who were increasingly taking on roles and functions providing government-funded social services (Gronbjerg and Smith 2021; Salamon 1995; Smith and Lipsky 1995; Wolch 1990). Integrated services would reduce the silo effect, such that networks of community services might treat their clients more nearly as whole persons while offering them less baffling points of entry into the system of social services. Results accountability would provide a form of transparency to ensure a more effective and efficient use of public funds, reconciling local flexibility with the need for rational-comprehensive planning by central authorities.

Welfare reform legislation gave concrete expression to these reform goals, initiating more extensive collaboration among silo-spanning networks and more conversations among the leaders of government, business, and community-based organizations. At the same time, many of the command and control tactics familiar to older welfare bureaucracies persisted, creating an enormous staff burden. Local welfare-to-work officials we surveyed estimated that local staff spent approximately 40 percent of their time on federal and state compliance and reporting requirements (Campbell, Lemp, and Trieber 2006, 7). Remarkably, roughly two days of every five-day work week were being devoted to activities other than providing direct services. As one local workforce director put it:

> I've been in this long enough to know that these block grant programs start off with a promise of minimal federal and state involvement, and then across the years, it creeps in. So we're seeing that. As you near the end of the life of a program, we're ever more burdened with more federal prescription, more state prescription, et cetera. There are too many deadlines, too much

oversight, too much disorganization at the state level, and too many stupid rules.

In this policy environment, there arose numerous occasions where what was needed to optimize the work of a local network came into conflict with received policy directives, agency rules, or formal accountability metrics (Behn 2001; Campbell and Glunt 2006). Welfare reform thus provided an ideal policy setting to learn about the tensions between metrics and mētis—between bureaucratic mandates and community-generated strategies—and the ways local implementers were coping with their contradictions.

As Kettl (2000) reminds us, public agencies were designed according to traditional ideas about bureaucratic hierarchy, and the legal infrastructure undergirding public administration still presumes this model. But contemporary administrative practice increasingly occurs in a system of network governance, where horizontal collaboration is the driving force. Citing welfare reform as a case in point, Kettl notes:

> The federal government "ended welfare as we know it" by passing the job to the states. The states, in turn, have typically devolved the task to their counties, and the counties in turn have contracted for-profit and nonprofit organizations to deliver welfare reform and, in some cases, to serve as managing contractor for the entire effort. Moreover, welfare reform is really a multi-faceted connection among job assessment, job training, job placement, and family support programs. Effectively managing welfare reform requires tightly coordinating these different programs—each often managed in turn by nongovernmental contractors. The result is an extended chain of implementation. A vastly complex network produces the program, and no one is in charge of everything. (492)

Local leaders we interviewed took the structural reality as a given, choosing to frame the governance challenge as a problem of management or, alternatively, of community development. Advocates of the former emphasize the need to bring fragmented workforce development and social service programs together into a more coherent whole, informed by outcome metrics. Proponents of the latter stress that "we can't succeed unless we get the whole community involved," taking advantage of local knowledge and calling upon community pride and civic-mindedness. In fact, the work requires an adept knitting together of both approaches, each of which has strengths and limitations.

The California Context in Which Reform Unfolded

In California communities, new governance reforms landed on local governments that were experiencing an ongoing fiscal crisis, the lingering effect of Proposition 13's restrictions on their ability to raise tax revenue. For the voluntary sector, they landed as the number of nonprofits was proliferating, the competition for funding was intensifying, and traditional funding stalwarts like the United Way were shifting away from providing unrestricted funds in favor of discrete grants accountable for predetermined results. At the same time, nonprofits were increasingly being called upon to deliver government-funded social services, a trend that subjected them to even more rigid results accountability requirements (Kearns 1996). This in turn led to dilemmas created by the competing ideals of vertical accountability and locally attuned decision-making.

Those dilemmas were front and center in the "placemaking" strategies that California foundations were adopting during the time of my fieldwork (Fehler-Cabral et al. 2016; Giloth 2019). This approach to philanthropy attempted to wed the ideals of results-seeking "impact investing" with that of giving the poor a voice, often in initiatives that were considered a long-term partnership between the foundation and the community. In contrast to the often top-down government funding strategies, foundations opted for a more grassroots approach, hoping to promote civic engagement so that communities gained the power to make a difference on the issues affecting them. Further, foundations nominally committed themselves to "approaches that are nimble, iterative, and responsive to the changing needs of a 'place' over time" (Fehler-Cabral et al. 2016, 84).

To one degree or another, and with widely varying degrees of success, these ideas shaped all four of the foundation-funded case examples discussed in the following chapters (see the list in the Appendix). As Nina Eliasoph (2011) has so vividly documented, the joint appeal to community empowerment and results accountability can create as many problems as it solves:

> Running from the bureaucrat's ghost solves some problems but causes others. . . . Managing, controlling, planning, measuring, paying: the ghost's work continues, but in new, different forms, with new, different consequences. . . . Cheerleaders and critics share a presupposition: a deep faith in a community that they imagine to exist before the nonlocal, non-grassroots influences arrived—a noble local community, better than bureaucracy and easy to disentangle from bureaucracy. The case of Snowy Prairie's youth programs shows just how untrue all that can be. (242, 243)

Around the time my fieldwork commenced, the conversion of nonprofit hospitals to for-profit status resulted in the creation of several very large private foundations in California. For example, the California Endowment is a private grantmaking foundation created as part of the conversion of Blue Cross to for-profit status in 1996. It launched with approximately $1 billion in assets, declaring its mission "to improve access to affordable, quality health care for underserved individuals and communities and to promote fundamental improvements in the health status of all Californians." The endowment adopted a community-based orientation to its work and has been particularly concerned with promoting the concept of a healthy community in disadvantaged areas. By definition, newly created philanthropies like the endowment had limited expertise in community grantmaking and faced a steep learning curve, hampering their initial efforts to ensure the grants were targeted appropriately and evaluated effectively.

Into this existing pressure cooker, welfare reform and its dramatic reworking of the terms of federal support for the poor raised anxieties in local communities. California state officials had deliberately devolved many important decisions to the state's fifty-eight county governments, the social service providers of last resort in the California system. Those counties featured widely varying political cultures and highly uneven capacities to plan and implement the new reforms. A single county, Los Angeles, accounted for roughly a quarter of the state's welfare recipients and funding, while many rural counties had much smaller recipient counts but also very limited staff and community capacity to manage change. In many rural communities, the local branches of organizations like the Salvation Army or Catholic Charities became an important supplement to government programs as a way to deliver social services. Devolution thus meant different things in different places. That reality, along with the new system's emphasis on creating individually tailored employment plans for welfare recipients, also made it harder for advocacy organizations, who had to adjust their strategies and roles.

Just as the community contexts in which our field research took place varied widely, the hidden heroes we interviewed did not fit any single mold. They held positions in a variety of local organizations and were engaged in different types of grantmaking relationships. They also occupied diverse positions within bureaucratic hierarchies or community networks or—as we will learn—within both simultaneously. What they shared was a set of recurring dilemmas around culture, rules, and scale, to which we now turn.

II

Hidden Hero Stories

3

Reconciling Bureaucratic and Community Cultures

As a community organizer within the Industrial Areas Foundation (IAF) network, Jerry's job was to build powerful people's organizations with political clout. In a heavily urban county, he used the IAF organizing model to assemble a coalition of more than thirty religious congregations from low-income neighborhoods, along with an important labor union. Capable of turning out hundreds of voters in local elections, the organization's rallies became must-attend events for politicians seeking endorsements, providing they were willing to publicly commit to the group's concrete policy demands. That agenda of community concern, emerging after a campaign of one-on-one house meetings and active listening to residents' needs, became the blueprint for demanding resources from elected officials and government bureaucrats. The language of political power was a shared currency among these would-be civic partners, but it only went so far in enabling them to join forces and implement programs of public value.

At the time welfare reform was rolling out in the mid-1990s, Jerry's organization sought a way to be proactive. They did not want to wait for churches to become social service providers of last resort. Jerry viewed typical workforce development programs as a dead end since they came without the promise of well-paying jobs with health benefits. Instead, his organization negotiated hiring agreements with local health-care providers who needed nurses and who paid a living wage. With these agreements in hand, he then approached public agencies who controlled the funds for job training, childcare, and other support resources needed to move low-income residents into good jobs. As Jerry put it: "The hiring agreements created opportunities for negotiation with the welfare department. It helps our congregations be viewed as institutions of power in the neighborhood." As a result, residents identified through the IAF network received priority access to the very limited pool of local job-training opportunities.

Jerry was partnering with bureaucrats to secure results of public value, but he had relatively little respect for them as a group: "Welfare bureaucracies are not conducive to innovation, no matter how visionary their leaders may be. The bureaucracy for welfare is going to be tough to move. They are well-meaning people, but the social workers they hire are exactly the opposite of the kind of people we want to hire. It's like a whole different world." At the same time, Jerry realized that the system in which the bureaucrats work limits what they can do: "They don't get any extra points or extra funding for putting someone into a good-paying job as opposed to just any job. And that's what we can make happen. We also provide some political cover for the reformers inside the system."

We spoke with one of those reformers two years after our conversation with Jerry. From Charlotte's vantage point as a manager in the local employment and training agency, she offered a mixed assessment of the partnership with Jerry's organization. "Their key strength is in using neighborhood churches and other neighborhood organizations to take the message to politicians. That's their strength, and it does get the attention of the politicians. The corresponding weakness is that they are perceived as doing good programs even when they don't do good programs. I'll leave it at that."

Her point was that the sought-after employment outcomes would not have been possible without the program management expertise her agency provided. Those who ran those programs were the social workers and bureaucrats whom Jerry held in low esteem. On the other hand, Charlotte knew that without the pressure Jerry's group applied, the welfare department likely would have defaulted to funneling clients into employment opportunities at the lower rungs of the job market. Instead, working in partnership, the bureaucrats and community organizer were able to creatively link potential workers to the types of well-paying jobs that were available locally. The skill sets required to reform bureaucratic systems from the inside are very different from those Jerry seeks when hiring organizers, yet both were necessary. The places where these worlds meet are full of possibilities but also tension. To get the attention of bureaucrats and politicians, community organizers like Jerry often adopt a confrontational style. Inside reformers welcome the organizer's ability to exert pressure on the system, but they bristle when it is they themselves on the other side of tense negotiations. As Charlotte put it:

> When they first came in, it was like union versus management. They would have their agenda all worked out in advance. Take it or leave it. And we work in a little more laid-back style here, more collaborative. More like, "Tell me what you want, and then let's figure out how we can do it." So there was a level of uncomfort when they came in with their implied threat of power. After a few meetings it began to get a little easier.

As any traveler abroad knows, navigating a foreign culture and language requires patient, relational work grounded in democratic sensibilities: curiosity about the other, humility about one's own ways, patient persistence as translation efforts slowly unfold, and a willingness to experiment and learn. Inserting those traits into time-bound, outcome-driven public grantmaking processes is no simple matter. Often it doesn't happen at all, as we found in evaluating California's workforce development system.

Culture Clash in the Workforce System

On beginning our evaluation of the California workforce development system, we found it riven by a fundamental culture clash. State Employment Development Department (EDD) officials are responsible for ensuring local compliance with federal and state rules and regulations. Local area workforce leaders are responsible for designing programs that are adapted to local circumstances and needs. These two imperatives often leave the parties working at cross-purposes.

The state agency is perceived by many local stakeholders as a rule-bound bureaucracy intent on telling people what they can't do. A local administrator describes it this way:

> EDD, if you follow it, is a very structured outfit. They've had so many rules which are so specific that they're not very useful. They don't just roll up their sleeves and say, "Let's go get 'em, Tiger, because this needs to be done and we'll explain it later." They do not have that attitude. . . . Now, we've had some real good luck locally, with local EDD people just really wanting to help out and get involved, but they pretty much have to disguise what they're doing to the supervisory chain up the ladder because they're not supposed to be doing that.

The latter half of this comment echoes a large number of comments we heard that reflect the great esteem in which many *local* EDD staff are held by their local workforce development partners. One of the workforce contractors expressed her sympathy for EDD employees who are doing their best to help but are hampered by their own organization:

> We're partners. They've tried really hard here locally to provide support to us, and vice versa. We have good local folks, but they're not allowed to do anything. You know, every single decision about the simplest thing has to come out of Sacramento, and I feel for them. They want to be partners, and they live in this town; these are their neighbors, and they aren't allowed to do anything.

Many interviewees use terms like "flexible" or "responsive" to describe what they like about their local EDD representative. By contrast, some of the state EDD personnel with whom they interact are seen as difficult partners:

> They're so departmentalized that when you're negotiating a lease, you're dealing with probably eight to ten different peo-

ple. And they come as a task force. They've got their management information system person, the furniture-moving person, the supply person, the building person that inspects the building for required measurements, an ADA [Americans with Disabilities Act]-compliance person; you have all these different people that are just so specialized in one thing, and then they want to drive it; they want to tell you what the lease should be; they want to tell you how much they're going to pay you.

From the state perspective, there are certain requirements built into the legislation that must be implemented with regularity and precision. Results accountability requirements, which at the time included seventeen mandated performance measures, are defined at the federal level and are tied to a range of discrete funding streams. As one state administrator put it:

Performance standards drive policy, and should, because the old saying is correct: "You get what you measure." When the locals complain about these measures it's a bit of whining. . . . We have no choice but to enforce these requirements. And we go out of our way to help locals navigate any changes that come about because of new legislation or regulations. We also carefully negotiate specific performance standards with local areas based on their demographics and economics. These negotiations take place every year.

This same administrator makes it clear that she has the final say after negotiations have taken place: "I have the authority to make the decisions on the local performance level. It would be a mess otherwise." She notes that she used to travel to local areas to conduct the yearly negotiations but because of funding restrictions on travel now conducts the exchange via email.

The time and resources needed to build productive relationships across the boundary where bureaucracy and community organizations intersect is in short supply. Yet there are good reasons to believe that such an investment is just what we need to produce the policy results we desire. Our next example provides a case in point.

Governance Work as Cultural Translation

The California Employment Development Department headquarters occupies a 1950s-era, six-story building just two blocks from the state capitol in Sacramento. A city street bisects the building's bottom two floors, dividing them with lanes of traffic. The top floors have hallways that run uninterrupted for two long city blocks. Walking the building's corridors in the mid-2000s, I looked in vain for a single sign of individuality such as a cartoon on a door or a piece of art on the walls. The building's architecture and ambience are in keeping with a certain ideal of neutral, professional, and uniformly delivered service.

That ethic pervades the organization's culture, even if it no longer defines the cutting edge in social welfare policy. The old adage about form following function is one explanation. One primary task of the department is to issue unemployment insurance checks. The workload is enormous and complex—requiring that (1) linguistically and cultural diverse individuals can make claims, (2) the system can distinguish legitimate from illegitimate claims on the basis of complex regulations, (3) accurately calculated checks reach beneficiaries in a timely fashion, and (4) an enormous human and technological infrastructure is maintained so that the system runs smoothly.

It is not the kind of place that tolerates mistakes. Not long before we began to evaluate an EDD program, a simple clerical error in one unit led to the miscalculation of thousands of unemployment checks, costing the state millions of dollars and untold time to fix, while opening the door to legal claims. Not surprisingly, the effort to do everything "by the book" is a sacrosanct organizational norm. When problems arise, the reflex of managers is to tighten up rigor and strictly enforce compliance.

Welfare reform and workforce development legislation in the 1990s forced the department to rethink old ways of doing business, a reform mode that conflicted with its organizational culture. In the early 2000s, the administration of Governor Gray Davis lobbed a policy grenade into this already-bubbling cauldron, directing the department's leaders to implement a community- and faith-based initiative whose design posed a direct challenge to the culture of risk avoidance (Campbell and Lemp 2007). A portion of the department's funds that would normally have flowed to state and local workforce programs was redirected to forty nonprofit community- and faith-based organizations, including many that had not previously received a government grant.

The initiative had two stated goals: (1) to expand access to workforce development services among hard-to-employ populations that were not well served by the existing system and (2) to build the capacity of participating organizations to function effectively as government workforce development partners. The civic goals were articulated by a top Davis administration official: "We wanted to get public resources deeper into communities where they would more likely reach poor citizens and structurally marginalized workers, providing jobs that would get them out of poverty. I wanted neighborhood organizations to be stronger after we left."

Jo, then the executive director of one of those first-time nonprofit grantees, is many things—aging hippie, community activist, born-again Christian, recovering drug addict, and former county government employee. But she is no one's image of a bureaucrat. Her conversations are littered with confessions of weakness or failure. She admits that she "has trouble with that whole accounting thing" and has no hesitation about informing you that for every successful participant in her drug recovery program there are three failures. In her world, mistakes are an expected part of a twelve-step-inspired cultural practice of admitting flaws, learning, making amends, and moving on—with larger or smaller portions of relapse and denial complicating the path forward.

Jo's swashbuckling style stands in stark contrast to the careful plodding of the sober Sacramento bureaucrats. But their paths were about to cross, just as she was transitioning what had started as a personal ministry into a fledgling nonprofit organization eligible for grant funding. The funding amounts flowing from the state initiative were not trivial: her nonprofit eventually received nearly half a million dollars over a three-year period.

The Translational Work of the Special Projects Team

The job of translating between the cultural worlds of local faith-related organizations and the state bureaucracy was assigned to the EDD's Special Projects Division. With the backing of the governor's office, their staff strove to wed government resources and formal requirements with the particular strengths and community connections of local nonprofits.

It was not easy. Even after two or three years of intensive work, many of the nonprofits still lacked certain capacities routinely expected of EDD grantees. Many EDD officials and staff were opposed to the whole idea of working with community-based organizations. "Why do it?" they would ask. And getting local workforce officials to welcome these groups as partners was an uphill battle from the start. As Molly, a Special Projects leader, explains: "I can see why some people would wonder if this is actually cost effective from a public investment perspective. Our team can see that what these organizations do is unique and reaches people our governmental system fails to serve, but it can be hard to convince others in EDD."

Our evaluation provided considerable evidence that the program did expand the reach of workforce development services as intended, reaching individuals with histories of drug use, incarceration, or checkered work experiences (Campbell and Glunt 2006). The Special Projects team played a pivotal role in doing the navigational work required to make the beneficial outcomes possible. Negotiating accountability requirements with grantees was a key challenge they had to meet.

In theory, results accountability is not like a financial audit or a compliance check. Rather than being concerned with small errors in process, the focus is on the outcomes. In practice, process accountability requirements do not go away. EDD staff had to navigate a fairly traditional set of top-down compliance measures while simultaneously layering on specially designed outcome expectations tailored to the unique capacities of each faith-related-organization grantee. In a departure from traditional practices, the state team built ongoing relationships with each grantee, nurturing their capacity to meet stringent reporting requirements and to operate within church-state legal restrictions. As Molly put it: "We went to them, which is not how EDD typically does business; it's always 'come to us.'"

Many tensions had to be navigated. Defying common sense, a grantee that provided work clothes to a large number of participants in encounters that typically lasted a single hour faced the same paperwork requirements for each participant as organizations that serve a handful of participants intensively over months or years. Other grantees found that standard eligibility restrictions, such as those excluding services to undocumented immigrants, ran against their open-door ethic.

In the face of these grating regulations, Jo and other grantees noted how patient the state program managers were in introducing and explaining the complicated rules. A self-described political conservative from a faith-related organization told us: "If all government programs were this responsive to local organizations, I'd be a lot more supportive. We were asked to change some of our internal policies to be in compliance with church-state guidelines, which we really didn't want to do. But we agreed because we believed in what this program was trying to do and appreciated all the people we were dealing with."

Bridging cultures proved particularly difficult with grantee organizations who had never previously received a government grant. An original Special Projects staff of six swelled to fifteen to keep up with the workload, operating less like a government bureaucracy and more like a nonprofit resource or technical assistance center. Grantees needed help developing strategic plans, thinking through staffing options, and developing sound accounting practices.

As Molly describes it: "You know, people worry about proselytization by faith-related organizations, but that's not the major issue. The worst part is that organizations go into business without any accountability in place for taxpayer dollars." This mantra of "protecting taxpayer dollars" is ubiquitous in social service programs, but efforts to calculate a bottom line in the traditional business sense run into inherent difficulties. As another EDD program manager put it: "What price do you put on having a family reunited? Someone who has lost a mother or father to drug abuse or whatever, when you put them back together, what price is that? Is that a $1,700 placement? Or is it a $4,000, or a $10,000? . . . If we help someone become self-sufficient now, who knows how much we might be saving in future social service or prison costs."

Adopting a Flexible Approach to Results Accountability

The EDD team did their best to deflect costs that the grantees otherwise might have faced. For example, they deliberately treated the initial compliance audit as a learning experience rather than an occasion to call out failures to meet the usual standards. Subsequent audits could focus on identifying real breeches of responsibility rather than simply picking up errors due to inexperience.

The flexible approach to results accountability was particularly important given the goals of the initiative. Historically, federal performance standards had led to "creaming," as government workforce programs did not enroll harder-to-employ clients who were likely to depress their outcome metrics and jeopardize future federal funding. This was among the problems that the governor's initiative was attempting to solve.

During the first year of the initiative, the EDD team exempted grantees from meeting federal performance requirements because they were funded out of state general funds rather than Department of Labor workforce allocations. When the federal funding and requirements kicked in during the initiative's second year, participating organizations were required to incorporate federal *eligibility* standards and to report on federal performance measures, but the state team and the leaders of each funded organization sat together to negotiate a unique set of performance benchmarks to which grantees were going to be held accountable by state officials. Many of these benchmarks were designed around organizational capacity-building goals. In the same conversations, program managers stressed that grantees needed to develop systems that could demonstrate measurable employment results if they hoped to attract future grants.

The practical accommodations allowed the partnership to move forward. Although the adjustments to standard procedures by no means satisfied everyone, they created a space for experimentation and learning. Part of that learning was about what might count as a viable result. Local nonprofit directors like Jo measured participants' success in small steps and in ways that administrative data fail to capture, such as "whether a participant calls us when they can't make an appointment" or whether they "keep coming back" even when a job is not immediately forthcoming. The outcomes that mattered to these organizations were expressed in terms that don't immediately translate into standard employment metrics, such as "giving clients hope," "building self-esteem," and "creating a sense of family." In response, an EDD official noted, "We need to develop a system of metrics to define the meaningful accomplishments of community- and faith-related organizations in the areas of preemployment." The two parties were still talking in different languages but were beginning to appreciate what each brought to the partnership.

Drawing on their community connections, low staff-participant ratios, and ethic of care, organizations like Jo's were building a ladder of incremental steps to link the world of poverty to the world of work. They excelled at the lower rungs of the ladder, instilling trust, confidence, and social skills that prepared participants to enter or reenter the job market. But the faith-related organizations had less capacity to provide the education and training needed to find a better job, something that government workforce programs had the resources to support. The relational work the nonprofits excelled at often presumed that they could hand off to government programs their more successful participants, who were now ready for traditional workforce services. Working together, the two parties could achieve results that neither could achieve alone.

In the case of Jo's organization, the state initiative provided the impetus for infusing her vocation of ministry with a strong complement of professionalism. She credited EDD technical assistance with helping her organization grow from a small grassroots group to what has become a large and effective social service organization. At the height of its faith-initiative grant, in 2005, her organization had the equivalent of eight and one-half paid staff (some worked part-time) and sixty program participants. A 2016 follow-up study found it had grown to forty-eight full-time or part-time staff and a budget of approximately $1 million per year (Campbell 2016). Local workforce officials note how it has evolved from "one of those church groups" ignored or sneered at in meetings to become a key provider of drug and alcohol recovery services in their county.

The EDD Special Projects team built a cultural bridge with community organizations from their location in a central bureaucracy. We now turn to an effort to build a similar bridge from below. The foundation-funded project was designed to elevate the voices of parents and community residents into policy discussions. Specifically, it sought to insert "lesser heard voices" into local commissions charged with deciding how funds intended to benefit children ages birth to five would be used (Campbell 2010).

Civic Engagement Where Cultures Meet

Daniela had been asked to give her county's Children and Families Commission an update on the civic engagement work she was leading. She brought along a group of parents she had been getting to know in community dialogue sessions. Her goal was to make commissioners aware of the day-to-day struggles facing local parents. She described the challenge as follows:

> The commission is very business oriented; they like to complete their business quickly. Most of them are leaders of big organizations and are used to doing things in a formal way. The challenge is helping them to slow down and think about the deeper issues so they make better decisions.

One of the parents, a teenage father, was very nervous about speaking. He wanted to know if he was dressed appropriately, where he would have to stand, whether it would be at a podium—questions that reflected the distance he felt from the world of the commissioners. Eventually, he warmed to the occasion and felt good about the experience. Less clear was whether his remarks had made much of an impact, in part because they were not offered in reference to any immediate decisions the commissioners were facing.

However, later in that same meeting the commissioners expressed an openness to a half-day "mini-retreat" at which they might consider issues in more depth and outside of the formal setting of a business meeting. Daniela remarks:

> People always talk about educating the community, but there's a whole other side to this of educating policymakers about what is really happening. It's a slow process, but I try to take advantage of opportunities whenever they arise. In the beginning there was skepticism on the part of some commissioners that civic engagement was worthwhile. There was some arrogance, the belief that the best sources of information were expert sources. That wasn't shared by all of them, but you certainly heard it.

With some persistent prodding, we moved them to a point where they actually doubled the amount of money to support our civic engagement work. They said: "What will it cost to do this right? What is it that we need? Where can we find the funds to do that?" Ultimately, we need commissioners to see themselves as community members, and we need community members to see themselves as having a role at policymaking tables. One of my goals would be a more fluid meshing of participants from these two groups.

One practical step Daniela took was to bring together two different civic engagement committees that had been operating separately. One was a formal subcommittee of the commission, which conducted their business according to Robert's Rules of Order and consisted primarily of key insiders from prominent service delivery organizations. The other was an informal group to advise Daniela on ways to engage a wider range of community voices. The newly merged group began to meet once a month over lunch. Daniela structured the conversation to encourage the in-depth discussion she felt was missing at commission business meetings. A couple of commissioners regularly attended the lunch meetings. Daniela was encouraged when one of them, at a subsequent commission meeting, referenced an anecdote he had heard from a parent at a lunch session. Daniela puts such small victories in perspective:

How you define success in this civic engagement effort is tricky because it's a process. It's ongoing. There really is no end point. There is more to consider than one teen father telling you about his life. The fact is we've now talked with a hundred guys who are twenty-one and under, and they'll tell you the same thing. So our responsibility is to extrapolate from some of these individual stories into a bigger story that then joins with other data to make sure the commission has both types of evidence available as they make decisions.

At issue is whether the marriage of expert-generated metrics and slow, relationship-intensive mētis would influence the quick-paced decision-making of the commission. Daniela offers a cautionary assessment:

> I think we did well on sponsoring well-run community dialogues but less so on influencing how commissioners made funding decisions. That left many people feeling disappointed that their input had not been heard. This was especially true for the grassroots people, like the family childcare provider who needs a small grant to upgrade their facility. Most of them don't even have the capacity to absorb one of our commission-sponsored grants and manage it, so they're out of the game to begin with. And the reality is that not everything that is needed can be funded. But I also think we need to keep in mind a bigger picture—not everything we do is simply about influencing commission decisions; it's also about developing leadership in the community over the longer term.

Being "out of the game to begin with" speaks to the difficulty of the cultural bridging Daniela was attempting. Her most frequently used civic engagement tool was a community forum, often labeled a "community conversation" or "dialogue." These occasions provided an accessible entry point for diverse parents and community members, promoting inclusiveness and civil dialogue. They did less well in engaging differences of opinion by differentiating areas of consensus and conflict. That step, building consensus, requires more time and a willingness to work through conflict. Daniela opted to put the emphasis on hearing everyone out rather than on parsing ideas or moving toward group agreements. Overall, while the high-energy dialogues facilitated robust discussions, our evaluation team found relatively little evidence that these discussions affected policy or programmatic decisions.

The Goals and Approach of Foundation Funders

The failure to achieve significant policy influence for the "nonusual suspects" was not for lack of effort. Using ample foundation funding, a cohort of eight county commissions were part of the Civic Engagement Project (Campbell 2010), animated by three guiding principles drawn from the public deliberation literature, in particular from the Kettering public issue forum model (Matthews and McAfee 2003):

- **Inclusive participation:** create diverse participation in the work of the commission and ensure that "lesser-heard" voices are involved, while valuing diversity in geography, ethnicity, income, language, family characteristics (e.g., children with disabilities, homeless families, gay and lesbian parents), professional disciplines, organizational affiliations, and sectors (government, nonprofit, for-profit).
- **Civil dialogue:** create ongoing discussion that builds bridges between and within diverse groups and individuals while creating mutual understanding, respect, and a sense of common ground and shared commitment.
- **Policy influence:** link public voice to commission policies and programs while making the commission and its "organized publics" an advocacy force in the community.

The commissions hired outreach workers like Daniela with strong community ties to build relationships with particular groups—defined by ethnicity, class, neighborhood, or special interest (Campbell 2010). For example, eight outreach workers in one county, most bilingual Spanish speakers, conducted intercept interviews at locations like migrant housing units, preschools, shopping malls, and grocery stores. Another commission deployed a Spanish speaker to work in the heavily Latino east county area and a popular black pastor to work in a predominantly African American area. Still another county hired fifteen outreach specialists to reach specific groups such as the faith community or gay and lesbian parents, effectively overcoming language and cultural barriers and promoting more inclusive participation in commission-sponsored events.

More than just direct verbal translation was at issue, however. The concept of deliberation itself was interpreted through distinct cultural lenses. As Daniela remarked, "A dialogue is an intense personal encounter with someone you trust." Given this assumption, she spends much of her time cultivating personal relationships. She framed her work within a "personalist politics" framework, in which the emphasis is less on organizing to promote citizen voice amid complicated organizational processes and more on sparking committed action by individuals or grassroots groups.

When we interviewed the outreach staff who had been hired with foundation funds, they described themselves as being caught between two very different cultural worlds, one heavily bureaucratic and formal and the other dependent on trusting personal relationships. Compare the following comments, the first from an outreach worker and the second from a staff assistant to a county Children and Families Commission:

Outreach worker: You have to really get out in the community and talk with people. This commission just really doesn't have a good understanding of what is going on with people. It was real frustrating for me. I am not easily intimidated, so I talked up. But I got squelched a lot. Eventually I got some people to change their minds on some things. I think a lot of times people start into these things with a lot of energy but then they get caught up in all the refinements and restrictions of the position, and then they start looking at things from the top down rather than the bottom up.

Commission staffer: The problem is not getting money out the door; it's doing it correctly. First, what are we buying? Are there outcomes and indicators of value attached to what we're buying? Not counting widgets, which is a typical county system, like, "How many clients did you serve?" I don't care how many clients you served—did you serve them well? I want to know what I am buying for this money. How is it impacting children ages zero through five? We're not here to please everyone. Everyone has something that needs to be funded. But what are we going to solve? That, I think, is what is totally different from the foundation approach. Foundations get caught into this thing like, "let's do violence prevention," or "let's do literacy." All of a sudden they're doing a hundred things, and nothing is solved.

Both of these individuals are expressing legitimate perspectives, but you can immediately sense the chasm that separates their worlds.

Few of the outreach staff felt comfortable in both these worlds or had found a consistent strategy for bridging the two.

Ambiguous Outcomes from Civic Engagement

Typically, Civic Engagement Project–funded outreach workers defaulted to creating events with relatively homogeneous groups who shared a previous history. They felt that this was the best beginning point for involving unaffiliated parents and other lesser-heard voices, individuals who are often less comfortable expressing themselves in more formal public meetings. Initial phone calls to recruit participants sought to convey the overall objective of helping young children and asked about the community members' concerns as parents. In many cases, no mention was made of the commission itself or what it might do for them. Not surprisingly, many dialogue participants we interviewed never understood the link between the outreach staff or the community dialogues and the formal work of the local commission. Instead, as one participant put it: "The meeting stressed what we can be doing in our own neighborhoods, getting to know our neighbors' kids, smiling, and being friendly."

Daniela had a more ambitious agenda, but even it did not realize the goal of influencing commission decisions. "I see what we are doing is developing leaders in the community, activating individuals and groups that can advocate for the interests of young children and families. It's a longer-term strategy that may take five to seven years to show results, as individuals' leadership capacities mature. It requires that we prioritize nurturing the tissues of community." From the commission perspective, this long-term strategy was seen as defaulting on their charge to create tangible results in the short term, to actually "solve a problem."

For their part, public dialogue participants we interviewed praised the follow-up provided by outreach staff in terms of meeting minutes or notes. But they wished for more assurances that their ideas were going to be used by the commission. They even echoed the insider concern with tangible results: "What are the tangible outcomes? I know it's a political decision, but it would be nice to see the impact of our participation, some accountability. For example, 'Here is your idea, and here is how the commission responded.' I haven't seen anything tangible." These comments suggested that the gap between what some participants we interviewed wanted to see—short-term, tangible impact on the commission and visible community results—and the primary goals and strength of the dialogues—long-term leadership and constituency development.

Since it bears directly on how and when citizens and experts interact, we were interested in the methods outreach staff used to communicate the views of dialogue participants to commissioners, which included staff reports, presentations by community members at commission meetings, and invitations to commissioners to be present at civic engagement meetings. None of these methods was judged to be very satisfying either by civic engagement staff or by commission executive directors.

Commissioners we interviewed put the most stock in occasions where they heard stories directly from members of the public, particularly encounters that opened their eyes to social realities from which they are distanced: "I get trapped in my own world, and it really helps me to connect directly with different folks in the community from time to time." From their vantage point, being an expert carried the accompanying cost of myopia. The stories of parents or other community members served to help them empathetically reconnect (Dzur 2019; Eckstein and Throgmorton 2003). Even here there are trade-offs, since the most meaningful encounters officials mentioned were ad hoc and not scripted, but these are by definition not as sustainable as having a regular, ongoing structure for interaction.

COVID, Food Insecurity, and a Hidden Hero Success

Our final case example in this chapter provides an encouraging example of bridging the cultural divide between bureaucratic agencies and community-based organizations. Food banks are in some ways a prototypical community institution, reliant on local donations and on a continuing supply of community volunteers. But during the COVID pandemic they forged an impressive partnership with public agencies, producing a result no one could have predicted.

An August 2001 U.S. Department of Agriculture (USDA) report (Coleman-Jensen et al. 2021) provided evidence that food insecurity rates in the United States did not increase during the first year of the pandemic, despite an economic downturn that drove unemployment levels to heights not even reached during the recession of 2008–2009. How was this unlikely result possible?

The beginning of an answer emerges from our study of the response of California's emergency food system to the pandemic (Meagher, Campbell, and Spang 2022).[1] The research found that, despite the unprecedented challenges, the overall response to the pandemic was highly successful, as suggested by both the USDA food insecurity metrics (Coleman-Jensen et al. 2021) and by the comments of our respondents. One opined: "I'm going to say this with humility. We thrived." Another noted: "I don't think the government and nonprofits have ever worked so close and so well."

Driven by the urgency of the situation, food banks rallied their local networks and adapted their procedures on the fly to meet the new demands. Yet their ability to do so was also crucially reliant on the timely provision of new programs and resources from federal, state, and local bureaucracies. The existence of a nonprofit intermediary, the California Association of Food Banks, also played a key role in linking local food banks to government resources. Overall, the response became an exemplary model of what bureaucracy and community networks can do when they work together to achieve a civic purpose.

Like the workforce development system, the emergency food system in California is a complex network of public and nonprofit organizations. Food banks play an important role as regional hubs that source and distribute food to partner agencies within a specific geographic area. These partners include food pantries and soup kitchens run by nonprofit organizations that distribute food directly to people who need it. Food banks typically procure food from a variety of sources, including donations from grocery stores, manufacturers, distributors, growers, and private households. They also rely on government programs—such as the Emergency Food Assistance Program—and in California, on the Farm to Family Program of the California Association of Food Banks.

As one might expect, the pandemic-related challenges facing the emergency food system were significant. Compared to pre-pandemic levels, most food banks reported serving double or triple the number of people during the pandemic. Widespread job losses led many people to seek help from food banks for the first time, especially people in the tourism or service industries, which were hit the hardest by California's stay-at-home order. As this demand for food was surging, food banks suffered significant drops in the volunteers—many older and thus more at risk from COVID—on whom they typically rely.

A food bank representative noted: "Every aspect of our operation literally changed overnight. You couldn't have people working side by side. Eventually we had more food coming in, and we didn't have the labor to process it." In response, Governor Gavin Newsom deployed the National Guard in March 2020 to assist food banks (Office of Governor Gavin Newsom 2020). Many food banks testified that this saved them from limiting their operations: "The Guard has been a godsend. We wouldn't have been able to stay open."

Food bank respondents credited their success at responding to the pandemic to an organizational culture of flexibility, collaboration with other food banks and partner agencies, and lessons learned from previous disasters. Adaptive strategies at the local level included creating new drive-through distributions to serve large volumes of people with limited physical contact; establishing or increasing food-purchasing programs; and expanding operational capacity, including warehouse space, refrigerated storage, truck fleets, new programs, and information technology infrastructure.

At the same time, government support was critical for rapidly scaling up their operations to serve the unprecedented demand. Food banks received financial and material support from all levels of government. For example, the USDA Farmers to Families Food Box Program was an important source of food for many food banks. The program was operational from April 2020 to May 2021, during which over 174 million food boxes containing fresh produce, meat, and dairy products were distributed (USDA Agricultural Marketing Service 2021). It was universally praised by our respondents for its speedy response:

> They contracted awards on a Friday, and seven days later I had semi loads of beautiful produce packaged into boxes unloading from our dock. There's no way I could have done that. I couldn't have sourced the food. I couldn't have gotten the boxes to put the food into. I couldn't have gotten the labor to put it in those boxes. I couldn't have arranged the transportation. There's no

way in the world I could have done that in a month, least of all a week. But in a week, they delivered. When we look at the last months, I would say that that's probably at least a quarter of our volume has been through that program. And again, that program didn't even exist a year ago.

In addition to the National Guard assistance, California's state government offered several types of support to food banks, including food (through a state-funded emergency food box) and funding for capacity building. The state also released emergency funds to purchase food for needy Californians, and its partnership with a nonprofit organization enabled the resulting food box program to deliver the first boxes in under two weeks. The funding came from the California Department of Social Services (CDSS), eventually totaling $75 million. Logistical support came from the California Association of Food Banks (CAFB), a statewide nonprofit supporting local and regional food banks. Their prior experience operating the Farm to Family Program—which delivers fresh and shelf-stable foods to California food banks—helped CDSS deliver over one million emergency food boxes in the nine months following the state's shelter-in-place order (California Association of Food Banks 2021).

A California Association of Food Banks staffer notes: "[Farm to Family] was ready to go when this pandemic hit. In the first couple of days we shipped 80,000 boxes of shelf-stable food to pretty much every part of California." A local food bank director describes the program's benefits:

> We were really grateful at the speed and the scale of the state's response. Within weeks, they were procuring state-funded food boxes that the Department of Social Services had rolling around the state in partnership with the California Association of Food Banks. . . . Honestly, it's government at its finest.

In addition, many food banks established or strengthened relationships with county governments during the pandemic. This included new and somewhat unlikely partners, such as police departments whose officers provided security services at food distribution sites.

The multiple partnerships locally and beyond, coupled with heightened media visibility, enabled food banks to build wider networks of support and address the stigma surrounding food assistance.

Interviewees believed that the county's support for the food bank during the pandemic reflected a new appreciation for the services they provide. Some noted that these shifting perceptions allowed the food bank to coordinate with local agencies more easily than had been possible before:

> Last year, for the first time, the county gave the food bank money. We've never gotten county funding. Ever. So that was amazing. I think that they are kind of realizing, "Wow, you know, the food banks do a good job. They know what they're doing." I don't know what they thought we did, but: "Wow, you guys distribute a lot of food." We're food distributors. That's what we do. We can take free food, and we can stretch a dollar better than anybody. Better than any government agency, that's for sure. I think they're realizing that.

Obviously, the sense of urgency surrounding the pandemic brought special focus and attention that heightened the motivation for government bureaucracies and community networks to collaborate. Still, it took the dedicated efforts of hidden heroes to demonstrate what such partnerships can achieve. Difficulties do not disappear in these collaborations, and policy choices will always spawn winners and losers or a better fit with certain local objectives than others. But if you had established the goal in March 2020 of ensuring that food insecurity did not increase during the initial months of the pandemic, you could hardly have foreseen such an effective result (Neblo and Wallace 2021). It is an example of the type of civic purpose that can only be realized when the essential, and essentially incompatible, forces of hierarchies and networks, metrics and mētis, are reconciled by coordinated and effective public work.

Cultural Translation and Democratic Humility

The case histories in this chapter illustrate both the public promise and the difficult challenge of bridging bureaucratic and community cultures, with their distinct languages, routines, and ways of operating. The hidden heroes forge a path through a forest of structural contradictions. There is no cookbook or recipe to guide them through the trade-offs and paradoxes they encounter. Instead, they seek practical alignment in context-specific settings via ongoing experimentation, contestation, compromise, and working accommodation. They carve viable options out of the situation at hand using existing resources and doing so against the backdrop of bureaucratic institutions that alternatively embrace, resist, or refashion citizen voices (Hess 2007). There is a kind of catch-22 feature to this relational work across cultural divides. Without clear reasons to think a partnership will work, there is little incentive to invest the time and attention it takes to bridge cultures. Yet only with this investment can shared interests and complementary assets be discovered and put to practical use. It took some time for the meetings between the community organizer Jerry and the workforce administrator Charlotte to move beyond simple confrontation to a working accommodation and partnership. Deeply ingrained habits and prejudices stood in the way and might have derailed less persistent and committed partners.

Local faith-related organizations knew they could use the funding the EDD was providing, but it took them some time to realize that they also needed the various forms of technical assistance and support the Special Projects team could offer. Leaders in local workforce programs needed the nonprofit organizations to reach individuals their own programs were not serving. Yet it took time for them to shake off their resentment at having funds diverted from their own coffers and to see how the partnership could benefit their own public work.

Civic Engagement Project outreach staff never fully succeeded in bridging the divide between the formal culture of their commissions and the community voices they were lifting up in local dialogues. In working with the public, they prioritized creating safe spaces for parents and others to air their concerns. But this left them less able to articulate a forceful community consensus in terms that might move commissioners to shift policy. What victories they could point to remained on the margins, seen more as a promising step toward a hoped-for future than an immediate answer to the challenge. Their heroism took the form of persistence in light of dilemmas and trade-offs that made short-term success unlikely.

A certain democratic humility is essential in the space where bureaucratic and community cultures meet. A mark of this humility is the willingness to honor what is true from the other party's point of view even when that seems culturally at odds with one's own perspective. In taking up conflicts over rules in the next chapter, we encounter a different set of hidden hero practices, marked less by humble persistence and patient listening than by assertive inventiveness.

4

Adapting Rules to the Situation at Hand

Virginia was appointed head of her county's human services agency in June 1996, just before federal welfare reform legislation passed. "I should have bailed then," she says, laughing. She was an outsider to the system, which made the learning curve steep. But it also gave her the freedom to ask, "Why do we do that?" A colleague described her willingness to experiment:

> What I really learned from her, though, was not any of the how-to details; what I learned was how to think "big picture." The woman, she's just amazing that way. I just was so in awe of her, and she just seemed to have no fear; she'd try anything, just to see. And if it didn't work, then we'd change it. She relied on her staff to keep her out of trouble. But she also was just very good at not necessarily buying the first time staff said, "Well, you can't do that." She was good at saying, "Well, tell me why I can't do this. Show me where it's written. Where is this set?"

Virginia admits to being scared at the outset of welfare reform, given the dire-sounding information coming out of Washington, DC. After the federal legislation passed, she was disappointed that the California state plan provided no relief from the old system: "All the old procedures were simply laid on top of the new emphasis on employment. So our staff had to do more work. We had to learn how to chunk it down into manageable pieces."

In her previous job, Virginia's main interaction with community groups had been in trying to find sites for homeless shelters. The reception she received was typically hostile. As the county began its welfare reform planning, she went neighborhood by neighborhood and found a very different dynamic. "Before there were always complaints about people sitting at home collecting welfare. I never get that now. Public perception shifted dramatically." A key part of that changing perception came from developing a different relationship with the local business community. "We have given welfare a new face for business. Our agency is now a member of every chamber of commerce in the county. Part of our pitch is, 'Why should you go through 300 résumés when we can send you the best candidates?' So we start to be seen as a business support program."

Over time, Virginia grew excited about the flexibility the new system enabled. How she seized and exercised that flexibility is instructive. As an example, consider the following vignette.

Virginia was responsible for reporting metrics to state officials indicating how many Temporary Assistance to Needy Families (TANF) clients had been sanctioned under the rules of welfare reform. It was just one of a host of local welfare-to-work metrics she was required to transmit to the state regularly. Locally reported numbers could then be compared across counties and aggregated into overall state statistics. The purpose was to inform official judgments about how the welfare reform agenda was playing out on the ground.

But Virginia wore another hat as well. As someone respected broadly within the community social services network, she was the leader of a local collaborative that brought together government, nonprofit, and private sector leaders to discuss how best to serve the county's disadvantaged populations. Building trust and working relationships among members of the collaborative had taken a long time and required patient listening. Though gathered at a single table, participants did not think alike or share the same preoccupations. Virginia and other county government leaders were eager for community engagement and partnerships, but their time was often consumed with sorting out technical policy and regulatory issues with state and federal officials. Nonprofit leaders were glad to be welcomed to the welfare reform planning table but found the process chaotic and driven primarily by top-down directives few of them supported. Businesses appreciated being given a more prominent role in a conversation about government social policy, but initially were unsure what benefit, if any, the new reforms would bring to their bottom lines.

Early meetings of the collaborative had been particularly contentious. Some participants saw welfare reform as a threat to the community's already-tattered safety net, others as an opportunity to end client dependency and disrupt the intergenerational cycle of poverty. Eventually, however, the group had found its way to a surprising point of consensus: they did not believe that *any* welfare clients should be sanctioned, since this just shifted costs from the welfare program to other parts of the local network, such as food banks or homeless shelters. From their local perspective, the federal sanction rules were misguided and the sanction metric would not tell state officials what they really needed to know.

If Virginia failed to issue and report any sanctions, she risked reprisal from her bureaucratic superiors for failing to follow the legislatively enacted rules. If she did go forward with sanctions, she would lose faith with the members of the local collaborative, undermining the progress they were making toward becoming a more cohesive network. Whatever choice she made would put her out of favor with certain colleagues with whom she needed to maintain a working relationship.

Ultimately, Virginia devised a strategy that did not eliminate sanctions altogether but did go a long way toward limiting them. Taking advantage of the legislation's stated goal of aligning social and workforce development services with local business needs, she opted to work around welfare reform's "work first" requirement. That part of the new policy emphasized getting clients into "any job" as a first step, rather than first attempting to improve their work readiness. As Virginia put it:

> We need to do a little sidestep from "work first" regulations. We're going to have to be very quiet about doing it and not ask the state for a waiver. The reality is that the standard job search

doesn't work for everyone. We need to be seen as an ally of business. A good portion of our welfare population are folks that businesses will not want to hire; 25 percent or so have skill issues or criminal records that will make them unhirable. So we are not sanctioning right away but are granting amnesty. Instead of sticking to the letter of the law, we will exempt them from the work requirement first and worry about any consequences later.

Virginia's "sidestep" kept her in the good graces of both her state and local colleagues. It is the kind of practical accommodation that allows the governance process to move forward despite conflicts over goals or rules. As she puts it, "Over time our staff has developed an increased tolerance for ambiguity. I joke with them: 'Did we kill anyone?' If not, we can fix it."

Ambiguity and the Two Languages of Administrative Practice

The neutral bureaucratic expert—doing everything by the book—may exist as a cultural stereotype but does not describe local public managers like Virginia. Their days are filled with indeterminacy. Because operational rules often conflict with one another, they frequently fail to act as useful guides to everyday behavior. As a result, these managers routinely make discretionary choices amid considerable ambiguity. As Wolfe (1989, 229) puts it, "Legal rules, then, whatever they are supposed to be, turn out to be ambiguous, situational, personal, and contingent."

Results accountability demands exacerbate this challenge. The multiplication of required outcomes and indicators within and across agencies becomes both "internally contradictory and operationally absurd" (Behn 2001, 208). Paul Posner writes: "One of the leading misconceptions that federal officials make is that individual programs can be managed and evaluated in isolation from other federal, state, local, or private initiatives" (quoted in Salamon 2002, 527–528).

If we consider the issue from the perspective of nonprofit community organizations, we find similar difficulties. Those looking to the nonprofit sector to carry the weight of adaptive mētis on their own may find themselves increasingly disappointed. Rather than focusing attention solely on their program participants and community circumstances, nonprofit directors increasingly must take into account the goals and directives of their government and foundation funders. As these organizations have become more reliant on funding sources beyond the local community, they face increasing pressures to take on bureaucratic characteristics.

The increasingly blurred lines separating government agencies and their nonprofit partners constitute a long-standing and well-documented trend (Gronbjerg and Smith 2021; Salamon 1995; Smith and Lipsky 1995). Greater professionalization and specialization bring some benefits to nonprofits, of course. But they also pose many threats, including mission drift as the search for funding grows more urgent; or a shift in how clients are treated because of the rules attached to grants; or the possibility that their advocacy roles are undermined.

The local public managers and nonprofit executive directors we interviewed are neither heartless automatons who mindlessly follow the rules nor renegades deliberately breaking the rules at every turn. They are, in varying degrees, conversant in two languages. The first language is necessary to operate within vertical chains of command. It is steeped in metrics, rules, and standard operating procedures. These demand attention because they are directly linked to the provision of funding for their organizations. But they also need a second language to operate effectively within the horizontal networks in which they are enmeshed locally—partnerships, coalitions, and integrated services teams, among others. These horizontal relationships require knitting together the specific resources of different organizations to meet the particular needs of clients or the goals of local collaboratives. Network partners sometimes rely on quantitative metrics, but in pursuing goals, they also emphasize mētis, making a series of context-specific practical judgments and ongoing, on-the-fly adjustments.

Bilingual in this sense, the hidden heroes like Virginia experience ongoing conflicts between formal rules and informal "sidesteps"—between their organizational silo responsibilities and their local network loyalties.

Workaround Stories as Learning Opportunities

As my fieldwork progressed, I began to realize the ubiquity of work-around stories, like the "sidestep" story told by Virginia. These narratives provide an opportunity to learn how the hidden heroes cope with the governance tensions created by bureaucratic rules. Workaround stories were particularly prominent in our evaluation of workforce development programs in California.

The Workforce Investment Act (WIA) of 1998 updated federal workforce development programs to align with welfare reform. The legislation directed Local Workforce Investment Boards, each with membership that placed business representatives in the majority, to promote workforce system integration, overcoming service fragmentation by bringing together parallel, competing, or complementary local systems and programs. The ideal of integrated services was given a specific form in the legislation, which identified seventeen *mandatory partners* and recommended their *colocation* at One-Stop Career Centers, a central point of entry for anyone needing workforce services. The complexity of what was being attempted is hard to imagine. At the time of our workforce system evaluation, California had thirty-three separate federal, state, and local funding streams allocating $4–5 billion in support of workforce programs (California Budget Project 2005, 1, 4). Local workforce boards assembled resources from these diverse sources, each with its own rules, regulations, and reporting requirements (Posner 2009, 238).

The interagency One-Stop centers have characteristics similar to those of a distinct organization with its own internal rules, regulations, procedures, and processes. Yet their collaborative arrangements are interlaced intricately with the mandates, customers, and performance requirements of each partner agency (Bardach 1998). The overlapping rules frequently contradict one another. Said one local official:

> It would be a lot easier if the funding streams were simpler. As it is, we have to keep one eye on the clock and one eye on the funding streams. Sometimes the bureaucracies of each organization mitigate against the collaboration; these are the obstacles we try to overcome. If there is something we cannot do in

a partnership manner, it is usually because of somebody else's rules and regulations rather than our own recalcitrance.

While network management researchers often focus on conflicts *within local networks* (O'Leary et al. 2009, 12; Posner 2009, 241), they pay less attention to the equally important question of how local public managers navigate conflict between *the chains of command in their home agency* and the *priorities of community networks*. When commitment to the goals of a local collaborative necessitates the evasion of vertically imposed directives, a common managerial response is a workaround. An alternative to either simple compliance or overt attempts to change the rules, workarounds are informal, situated practices that typically attract little attention (Campbell 2012; Ferneley and Sobreperez 2006).

Workaround stories stay underground because of their informal, ad hoc character and their potential to expose local managers to reprisal from compliance-oriented superiors (Ban 1995; Campbell 2011a; Levin and Sanger 1994; O'Leary 2010; Storing 1980). However, by promising confidentiality and building rapport, our interviews created a safe space in which respondents shared a wide range of workaround stories. These five examples, shared by local workforce officials, give a flavor of their diverse forms:

- In dealing with mandated partner requirements, we are more flexible in order to be more strategic. Instead of trying to get the housing person the legislation calls for, which has been difficult, we find somebody who represents housing from another organization that wouldn't fit the letter of the law right now but would be a good advocate.
- If a person is a dislocated worker, just laid off or fired, and they had earned quite a bit of money—like the high-salaried people that make $80,000 and up—it's hard for us to enroll them because we can't meet the wage replacement performance measure. No matter what kind of training we give them, they're not going to start at that high level. The way we get around that is we tell them to go to a temporary agency, get any kind of job, and get a wage record with a pay stub.

Then we can use that wage as opposed to the previous wage in determining the wage replacement measure. So we tell them, "Go to McDonald's, flip hamburgers, but just get your wage down so we can bring you into the program."

- The Department of Labor and the General Accounting Office are claiming that the workforce system is only serving a couple hundred thousand people a year across the nation. But they are only counting those who are formally enrolled in training programs because no one in the system has come up with a way to capture data on the much larger number of people who use our system of universal services. Universal access was one of the wonderful ideas in the legislation, but we've had no leadership on how to gather data to tell that part of the story. So the whole program is undervalued and at risk of further federal funding cuts. So we've developed our own local tracking system.

- It's frustrating to spend all your time processing paper to make things work according to the rules and very little of your time getting people to work. . . . We got them [state and federal officials] to include money for postemployment support, which is critical to keeping people in jobs once they find them. But the fixes won't kick in until the day the rules say our yearly allocation should be totally spent. So we went ahead and just totally disregarded the rules and did it anyway. Eventually we will go back and make sure that everything pencils out.

- While we were working hard locally to get all the partners to work together seamlessly, the head of one state agency issued a directive that their sign would be out in front of the One-Stop, blazing away. Well, our folks put together a sandwich sign that they would put out in front only when state folks came down to visit . . . when they left, we put it away.

Some respondents recounted the problems created when rule-bound local managers refused to implement a workaround. For example, one local workforce board had to send $3.5 million back to the state as "unspent" because it had not been allocated by the June 30 end-of-fiscal-year deadline. In reality, the local area had not even received their state allocation until five months into the fiscal year, and many vendors were behind in delivering orders. This is a fairly routine occurrence that prompts most local fiscal officers to find creative workarounds. But this particular accountant chose not to do so in the name of strict compliance with the law. As one of his disgruntled colleagues put it: "How you interpret regulations locally can have a big impact. Believe me, if you are creative, you can drill holes in any set of federal and state regulations."

Managers often adopted broad, generic rationales to support the workaround posture: they emphasized how unique their local setting is compared to other jurisdictions or called selectively upon legislative language supporting local discretion. As one local workforce area director put it: "We try our darnedest to obey the law, but we have also found provisions in the law, especially the local flexibility clause, that allows us to do a lot of things for which others are still waiting for direction from the state. We don't wait." Another went even further: "We don't need new policies. What works is workarounds."

The most successful hidden heroes find creative approaches to wedding mētis-infused practical judgment with a realistic appreciation for performance metrics and formal rules. Here are four strategies they use to redefine the dilemma in practical, actionable terms rather than as an either-or choice between opposing principles:

- Establishing the goals of local collaboratives as an alternative locus of accountability
- Using performance to justify discretion and manage risk
- Treating rules and directives as starting points for negotiation
- Distinguishing front-door services from backdoor accounting

The stories told by a local workforce director in a rural region help convey what these strategies look like in a real-world setting.

Fitting Policy to Place

Sitting in his home office in a remote rural community, Henry took a great deal of pride in what he had accomplished over the past two decades. As the director of a local workforce development agency that serves a politically conservative region, he had won the respect of small business owners and local politicians, groups whose antigovernment views were deeply entrenched. He did so by bending the abstractly cast parameters of federal workforce programs to meet the unique circumstances of the local region. By means of a great deal of assertive and creative work—including many workarounds—Henry's team exercised democratic agency, aligning unlikely bedfellows in the pursuit of a shared civic purpose. It was a clear case of local discretion in implementing policy, but it also benefited from Henry's ability to maintain a professional working relationship with state workforce officials and compliance monitors.

The decline of the timber industry hit this region hard during the 1980s, removing one of the largest sources of well-paying jobs. The restructured economic landscape meant that small businesses were now the area's predominant employers, but government job-training programs had a bad reputation among their owners. This was not simply a matter of ideological opposition. An employer looking for a new office manager who contacted a workforce agency was once told, "We can't help you because none of those we serve are capable of doing the work you need done." At the other extreme, a company looking to fill a position with very specific job demands was once sent fifty résumés from everyone on the workforce agency's current list of enrollees, putting the burden of sorting through them completely on an already-stressed small business owner.

Henry and his team began exploring how they could better provide business services. A local workforce board member—herself a small business owner—said:

> If you're serious about that, help us with our human resource management. We're small businesses; we don't have an HR department; we hear horror stories of people getting $100,000 fines, losing their businesses, losing their homes, because they forgot to document something. We don't even know what is required, and we're afraid to ask because when we ask it will show that we're not doing it!

The board decided to make supporting the human resources needs of small businesses their primary mission. In effect, they were establishing the local collaborative and its civic goals as *an alternative lo-*

cus of accountability. They redefined—to the degree they could—state and federal bureaucracies as support structures for their local efforts rather than seeing them primarily as the master to be served. Henceforth, managers and staff in the local workforce area would begin to see themselves as accountable not only to state and federal program requirements but equally to local needs and demands. Noting how quickly staff responded to a local board member's information request, a manager explained: "Six or seven years ago, our staff response would have been, 'We don't collect that data because we're not required to.' Now, no one on our staff would ever dream of saying that to one of our local board members."

Over time, the workforce system in the region became the place to go for a wide range of business services. These included job posting, recruitment, labor law training, and related efforts for start-up businesses; business expansion efforts such as finding loans; and business closure activities that helped employers comply with federal regulations while helping dislocated workers take practical steps toward reemployment.

Not everything went smoothly during the transition. Local workforce officials had to win over not only the skeptical business community but also their own staffs, who were being asked to take on radically altered assignments and activities. A staff member told us: "Change is very difficult. Many of us who worked for years in the workforce system wondered if by serving business we were turning our back on the job seeker. There were a number of people who said, 'This is not going to work for me.' And they left."

Even more difficult was adapting the programs, funding requirements, and compliance demands of federal and state workforce bureaucracies in ways that made sense in light of the decision to prioritize small business needs. Unless one is immersed in the arcane details of this policy world, it can be hard to appreciate just how challenging this adaptive work can be. But our conversations with Henry provided numerous examples of how it happens. Here is one:

> You're supposed to be serving people that aren't already employed. Incumbent workers don't even count in the federal performance standards, there's no place for them, despite it being what our business customers want and what would ben-

efit their employees. So we said, "Wait a minute. We're going to have to break new ground here." We read all the regulations carefully and discovered there's this little thing called a "self-sufficiency standard"—you *can* train people that are already employed *if* they're not up to a basic level of self-sufficiency. Most local workforce areas put that standard at minimum wage, but we pushed it up to fifteen bucks an hour for our region. That means that we can serve most anybody working in our region. The state had a heart attack when I first told them how we were defining it.

In other cases, staying true to local priorities and accountabilities becomes a matter of not doing what the federal and state officials are emphasizing:

> There's such a mantra on training. The state wanted like a hundred percent retraining for everybody coming out of a timber mill closure. We're telling them, "A hundred percent of the people don't *want* retraining." About 30 percent of them will probably find another job in the same field fairly quickly just by relocating. Most of the people don't really want retraining; they're wanting to be reemployed. The state doesn't seem to understand that a one-year retraining class—it's very difficult for the average person to sustain their life while they're doing that.

For Henry, the key is staying true to the program's underlying purpose:

> There's a difference between people who are doing everything to support "the program" and people who are doing everything they can to support the customer. Especially as you go up further into the state bureaucracy, most people want to make sure that they don't get in trouble, so their whole life is spent trying to restrict what can be done.
>
> When we're breaking rules, it's not so we can get everybody on staff their own private car. It's so we can figure out how to provide better employer services or how we can train people who are already employed. Things like that are not well sup-

ported by the existing system but are essential in supporting small businesses who are the backbone of our rural economy. It all has to do with what the ultimate goal of the program was supposed to be, but because of the way that the rules are written and interpreted, it appears that you're not really allowed to do some of the very things that are most needed by businesses and job seekers.

Henry and his team managed to turn the basic results accountability formula on its head. According to new governance reformers, discretion is granted to locals as long as performance follows. But, in practice, *performance is actually a supporting cover that allows local discretion to be seized,* since compliance demands have not gone away despite the reforms. As Henry puts it: "In working around certain rules, you're betting that you won't get caught while you're still on the road to success. . . . But if you've already accomplished something, then it's much easier to defend."

Like most workaround practitioners we heard from, Henry keeps his workaround practices under wraps until he can point to performance improvements that justify deviations from standard procedures (Levin and Sanger 1994, 224; Storing 1980, 10). When auditors raise compliance concerns, he can respond: "Look at our results." Where local areas establish an ongoing track record of performance, state compliance officials who otherwise have cause to look with suspicion instead start to look the other way:

> What will happen is that you get a reputation over time. We play it pretty much above board as far as the details of what state monitors are looking for. It's not uncommon for us to fill out their monitoring guide for them. Makes life a lot easier for them. A lot of times when it comes right down to it, when you get the bureaucracy looking for it, it's a nitpicking kind of thing. And so you just take care of the nits for them, and they don't even look up to see what's going on out the window. You asked me how come the state doesn't come and kick our butts even when they know we're bending the rules like crazy. One reason is that we don't go *after* the state staff; we don't try to humiliate them. We don't try to blame them because we know that they

don't have any control over what they are asked to do. We treat them with respect.

Local public managers never know when a newly minted directive from a federal or state official will undermine some aspect of hard-won collaborative relationships. For example, the state director of a key partner agency may suddenly decide that because of budget cuts the agency can no longer colocate staff at the One-Stop. The randomness of such bureaucratic shocks can induce a sense of helplessness (Seligman 1975). In some managers, the repeated shocks lead to passive acquiescence—"Just tell me what to do, and I'll do it"—as with what Carolyn Ban (1995, 13) terms "demoralized managers."

But for others like Henry, it leads to *treating rules and directives as starting points for negotiation*. When this negotiation is conducted openly and formally, we are in the realm of requests for waivers or other formally approved local exceptions. By contrast, workarounds come into play because many managers view the effort to seek formal adjustments or exceptions as a waste of time, preferring to seek retrospective forgiveness rather than advance permission. As one of Henry's colleagues put it: "I can move a lot faster and get a lot more done if I don't have certain levels of approval process to go through. Many things are not fair if we follow the rules exactly."

Rules surrounding the reporting of employment outcomes are particularly problematic. Abstractly cast employment metrics obfuscate distinctions that are important in particular cases. I can get a job that does not pay enough to offset the new childcare costs I have to absorb. I can get a job that requires me to commute in ways that are taxing and costly to me and my family. I can get a job that is so beneath my talents that it is demeaning. I can get a job where the boss is abusive. I can get a job that does not pay enough so that I still must rely on some form of public assistance. The standard counter is that, for the unemployed, any job is a good first step. While no doubt true in some abstract sense, this argument ignores details that can matter greatly for particular individuals. As many local officials reminded us, official metrics do not tell us all we need to know if our concern is for the overall well-being of particular clients and communities rather than simply the functioning of the work incentive system.

Henry's team learned to *distinguish front-door services from back-door accounting*. They found ways to translate the local business-first priority into terms that met the federal expectations and performance standards. Indeed, their ability to document a public return on investment for every dollar they received became a model others in the state wanted to emulate. Henry notes: "We can show, conservatively, around $64 million in a combination of savings and increased income for our local businesses. At the same time, we can show a dramatic increase in job placements and training (primarily on-the-job training) for employees."

For a more cautionary tale, we turn to the story of a hidden hero who ran afoul of federal officials even though he was widely considered an effective and innovative public manager.

Rules, Silos, and Service Integration

Workaround stories lead us back to fundamental tensions and contradictions in what we want out of public policy. On the one hand, policymakers want the innovative use of local discretion to achieve service integration that saves money while benefiting citizens. On the other hand, decision-makers want greater accountability for, and control over, how public funds are spent. These competing rationales coexist uneasily, defining a structural tension with which local public managers cope daily.

We encountered a case in point during our research in a county known for its innovative approach to service integration. In leading that effort, Scott and his team identified 8,000 people in the county who were at risk of not being able to pay for rent or food:

> Rather than take the money welfare reform provided to develop a larger welfare program, we decided to develop a system that would integrate the resources we already have in ways that prioritized these families. By providing them services in a more structured and integrated way, we could focus on the outcome of self-sufficiency. The extra money welfare reform provided would be used to fill gaps in existing services rather than to build a completely separate system of services. Success would

be judged by how many families get employed in ways that move them into the middle class, in ways that are sustained.

Fiscal metrics played a key role in disciplining the new collaborations. As Scott put it: "Our bread and butter politically is the ability to say that our approach saves money."

Ironically, one of the efforts at service integration ended up costing the county millions of dollars in federal fines, having attracted the attention of a federal agency intent on ensuring that its funds were being used according to the strict letter of the law. Bureaucratic silos and funding streams do not go away when county-level administrators find creative ways to blend funds in support of individual clients. Any attempt to merge funding streams carries the accompanying risk of raising the concerns of compliance-oriented superiors in federal bureaucracies, who can scrutinize local actions for evidence that their funds are not being spent as intended. It can also spur local turf wars, as disputes arise about how funding integration might disparately affect different county agencies. While the turf wars appear on their surface to be local, they often have their origin in how funds are managed at the federal level.

In Scott's case, having promoted blended funding streams to facilitate "wraparound services," he rankled some local department heads who felt the new system would threaten their fiefdoms. Coincidentally or not, it also garnered the attention of federal authorities, when a whistleblower asserted that certain new billing practices were illegal. Fingers pointed in many different directions in trying to assess blame for the irregularities. An investigation determined that the issue stemmed from the simple failure to adopt a new federal billing form. However creative and necessary the local integrated services effort had been, the dispute not only cost the county a hefty fine but generated a host of negative publicity in local papers.

The complexity of the systems in which local administrators operate, and the ongoing possibility of encountering embarrassing press or political fallout if one strays from strict compliance, causes some administrators to attempt to do everything by the book. This rote stance is in turn what gives bureaucracies their well-deserved reputation as being rigid in ways that do not fit with local circumstances, the best interests of clients, or fiscal efficiency.

Workarounds and the Contradictions of Public Policy

The workaround stories of local public managers provided examples of marrying metrics with mētis, motivated by (1) developing and sustaining integrated services *partnerships* at the local level, (2) enhancing service quality and effectiveness for *program participants*, (3) adapting policy to unique local *community* circumstances, and (4) protecting *staff* time.

When a local public manager treats directives as a "starting point for negotiation," she has simultaneously accepted both the directive's validity from her superior's point of view and her own freedom to respond to it in terms not fully anticipated by the superior. If both her and her superior are committed to the practice of results accountability, this kind of back-and-forth can be an expected and respected way of doing business, and it can be disciplined by careful attention to whether particular acts of discretion produce the intended outcomes. If, instead, what is really going on is all about top-down control, the space for negotiation is closed off and the craft practice of results accountability is cast aside, even if something by that name is incanted. Similarly, if locals use workarounds simply to evade just rules or substitute private for public goals, they have stepped outside the container of results accountability as a disciplined way of thinking and taking action.

Workarounds and other forms of local discretion pose vexing dilemmas for democratic theorists. In his seminal work on street-level bureaucracy, Michael Lipsky (1980, 229) points to the essential conflict: "A paradox of public service provision in democratic societies is that policies must be administered fairly; similarly situated people must be treated alike. And yet . . . we also want our public services to be responsive to the presenting case." Robert Behn (2010, 1) captures the same paradox at the community scale: "To improve performance, public employees need to employ not impersonal rules but their personal knowledge of the specifics of local problems and the local conditions. . . . But discretion opens the door to reciprocity—and thus to corruption."

As a child of the southern United States who grew up while racist politicians were doing everything they could to evade federal civil rights protections, I am well aware of the perverse and undemocratic ends to which local discretion can be put. It can clearly be used to subvert the legitimate expression of public will via legislation or executive authority. On the other hand, without some flexibility to interpret rules and take local or individual context into account, centrally funded programs become blunt instruments. The backlash against mindless or rote bureaucracy is both a practical response to its dysfunctions and a legitimate source of democratic discontent.

We need new accountability mechanisms that can both honor and discipline local variation while promoting both transparency and organizational learning. But we also need the public to be more aware of the difficult bind facing local public managers and their partners, hopefully making them more forgiving of imperfections because they understand the challenging trade-offs being navigated. The reality is that we want different and sometimes contradictory things from government policy—including both creative service integration and strict accounting for the use of taxpayer dollars—not all of which can be easily achieved at the same time.

We now turn to a third important source of structural tension facing the hidden heroes, this one rooted in dilemmas of scale that arise when assessing project outcomes.

5

Traversing Scales in Assessing Outcomes

In August 1994, prison chaplain Veronica began one-on-one visits with women in a county jail. Seeking to counter high rates of recidivism, she and her husband, George, began helping the women find jobs and reintegrate into society upon their release. Inspired by a message received during prayer, Veronica began enlisting the women at the jail in helping her design a nonprofit organization to put her faith into action.

The model that evolved was built on the premise of ongoing peer-to-peer support rather than on a fixed, time-limited program. It begins by meeting each woman at the jail on the day of their release, providing them with toiletries and other basic essentials, finding them a place to live, and supporting their efforts to garner meaningful employment. The women are then invited into an ever-growing support network of women who have faced similar situations and challenges.

The nonprofit's "family," born when the first woman was picked up from jail in 1996, grew to include hundreds of women, many of whom meet for monthly potlucks that combine elements associated with support groups, twelve-step meetings, and church socials. As recorded in field notes from observing one of these potlucks, "There was a continuous hubbub of calling back and forth, hugging, much laughter and teasing . . . it was a ribald group, frank about topics like divorce or sex and unembarrassed to ask highly personal questions." At the same time, "a lot of practical information was exchanged: where to go to find this or that, what stores had the best prices, how to get an appointment with the dental service and what to expect there."[1]

For its first few years, Veronica's organization operated as a personal outreach ministry, sustained primarily by private donations and the volunteer efforts of the director, her husband, and some of the original participants. In April 2000, it incorporated as a nonprofit organization. Subsequently, it received and successfully managed a series of sizable government grants, beginning with a state faith-based initiative grant from the California Employment Development Department (EDD) (totaling $393,500 over three years). Even larger grants from other government agencies would follow, including projects addressing substance abuse and mental health.

We might expect that this organizational development trajectory would require sacrificing the peer support model in favor of something that seemed more professional or even bureaucratic. In fact, the organization managed to find a unique approach that blended the best of both worlds. Veronica excelled at inspiring women to take charge of their own lives, aided by the robust support of women facing similar challenges. George, a veteran of government social service programs, drew on his professional expertise to help the organization cope with the paperwork requirements of government contracting. He also helped it find its niche within the broader network of community services.

For example, George knew that their part of the county had historically been underserved in terms of government-funded social services and needed nonprofits to fill the gap. George's experience also made him aware of the wide array of local organizations to which their participants might be referred:

> We partnered with the local community college. I would tell our women, "Okay, if you want to go to school, now's the time to do it," because it's the one time going to jail will be a benefit since it means you didn't make any money last year and therefore will qualify for financial aid. So here's your tuition money;

here's your book money; here's a little bit of cash in your pocket. We've probably gotten about forty or fifty people into school this way. I know who to send them to at the school—"You can talk to this lady, tell her who sent you, and she'll know what to do; she'll understand."

For someone just out of prison, this navigational assistance can be critical in overcoming fears or the feeling of being overwhelmed, emotions that drive many back into drugs or alcohol. George notes:

Most of them are scared, you know, like, "What if I screw up?" And then when they find out "I can do this," they get such a surge of confidence. We do a lot of brokering of services. Anybody that will talk with me I'll network with, anybody that will get on the phone and let me say a couple of words and get a door open. So I'll send our folks to other places. We are one of the few organizations that can get them dental services. Or if they need an emergency meal or a one-night housing situation real fast, we'll hook them up with a church. And that's what makes us unique: we see people as human beings and touch them at that level, where they live, where it happens. My training is as a social worker and my work for forty years has been in social services, and I don't see that happening in a lot of places, that acknowledging of someone's humanity.

As a veteran of government, George has a nuanced appreciation for the motivations and stresses facing frontline bureaucrats in public agencies:

We are all hard on government, but there are a lot of people in government who go the extra mile, there's no question. But they have so much paperwork. You walk into a welfare office, and they have the bulletproof glass, and you walk up to the window, and there are fifty people in line behind you. You're trying to explain to them that you just need a little bit of help, and they hand you a stack of papers and say, "Fill these out and come back." For our population, a lot of them, they would just turn around and walk out and do what they know how to do, which is sell drugs, sell their body, do whatever it takes to feed themselves and survive.

When you work in one of those offices, it's like a mill because you've got so many minutes to process people, so you can't spend the time saying, "And how did you feel about that?" It won't happen. Somehow we've got to find a way to create more balance, to humanize it, and that's what we are able to do at our organization.

Veronica and George recognize the need to demonstrate outcomes of public value. They dutifully filled out the reports required by their government funders. But they also went above and beyond these routine exercises in accountability, which limit themselves to identifying self-reported results that can be tied to specific program interventions over the short duration of a particular grant. By contrast, their organization sought out an independent, longer-term study of the organization's effectiveness in reducing recidivism. Only 23 percent of their participants enrolled in the study were rearrested in the twelve months after their release, compared to an overall recidivism rate in California prisons of 66 percent (D. Miller 2009).

Veronica and George attribute their success to an ethic of care for particular individuals and an ability to effectively partner with a wide range of public agencies. Public officials we interviewed, including prison administrators, expressed uniformly high regard for the organization, citing the organization's demonstrated ability to deliver services and to navigate relationships with prison officials, social service agencies, and local employers. As evaluators, we found their success came not from a preset program but from (1) the ongoing community of support—a sisterhood—built among the women being served and (2) effective partnerships with public agencies.

Traversing Scales in Attributing Results

As we came to understand the work of the hidden heroes like Veronica and George better, our research teams found that we had to rethink what we paid attention to in conducting outcome evaluations. It was clear that standard program metrics failed to account for the importance of *local network dynamics* as generators of valued outcomes. That same narrowing of focus also failed to account for the role *participant codetermination* played in generating outcomes, independently of programmatic interventions. Both the local network and participant codetermination perspectives revealed the difficulty of balancing results metrics that inform short-run programmatic decisions with the reality that changing network relationships and participant behavior takes a *longer time frame*, well beyond what typical program metrics measure.

The most common scale for devising metrics of accountability is the program or project since this is how we typically allocate resources to solve public problems. This creates frequently recurring scalar-translation difficulties. First, program metrics do not tell us what we need to know about how individual programs fit with and contribute to broader community networks of services or to community-scale outcomes. Second, they fail to capture the important codetermination work of program participants and frontline staff, which can influence intended outcomes independently of programs, particularly in human services. Third, program metrics typically presume relatively brief time frames, failing to account for how short-term interventions fit into the broader history of community change efforts or contribute to long-term improvements in the lives of troubled individuals.

The hidden heroes like Veronica and George confront these scalar tensions regularly. The results reporting requirements they face presume a program-centric perspective. But when we asked them what was working to make results happen, they often told stories about network partners, participant codetermination, and community connections forged over time. Reconciling these perspectives requires an ambivalent posture toward standard results accountability requirements. They must be honored to provide what funders have a right to expect. At the same time, they cannot be allowed to cause implementers to neglect *all* the factors that actually create results. It is a tension to be managed rather than a problem to be solved definitively.

As evaluators we found ourselves in a similarly ambivalent posture. We were charged with assessing the effectiveness of particular funded programs or initiatives. But listening to the hidden heroes helped us to understand the limits of program-centric blinders and the need for a certain kind of evaluative peripheral vision.

Results as Network Products

In 1996, my colleague Joan Wright and I were invited to Humboldt County by the local Cooperative Extension office. We were asked to provide technical assistance to executive directors of nonprofit economic development organizations who were struggling to adapt to the results accountability demands that were increasingly attached to the grants they received. Aware that funders wanted to see evidence of results rather than simply documentation of how funds were used, local nonprofit leaders hoped to identify best practices for outcomes assessment in community economic development. The work was vital to the north coast region of California, which was attempting to transition from heavy reliance on the timber industry to more diversified economic development.

Our technical assistance team brought to the task the au courant tools of results accountability, including the use of logic models and a comprehensive list of economic development indicators. We engaged in three primary activities: (1) consulting with local nonprofit leaders to identify outcome-indicator pairs relevant to their particular economic development projects, (2) surveying community leaders and funders to identify community-level indicators they trusted, and (3) conducting a focus group that brought together funders and the nonprofit leaders to discuss questions and themes that emerged from the first two activities.

The project—conducted in partnership with a local Cooperative Extension advisor and a colleague from Humboldt State University—took place in a space that was free from many of the constraints, anxieties, and fears that accompany formal evaluations. In addition, the nonprofit leaders we worked with were highly motivated, skilled at what they do, and experienced as grant writers. Most had been with their organizations for many years, and many were involved with the local economic development forum. Even so, the project did not go as smoothly as we anticipated. The impediments proved instructive.

The first phase of our work—supporting their creation of project summaries and program logic models—took months longer to complete than planned. Project leaders found it very difficult to identify indicators that measured what they felt was important about their work. Adding to the complexity was that the projects often had multiple, nested goals and numerous organizational collaborators. If the outcomes were products of collaborative networks, it made little sense to attribute them to their organization alone. Indicators for project outcomes could be developed, but the challenge was to find indicators that (1) captured the complexity and uniqueness of the projects, (2) did not impose self-defeating costs to collect, and (3) made sense given multiple partners or funders with multiple goals and multiple accountability emphases.

Focus group participants noted that it is hard to demonstrate a measurable impact on a particular community goal as the result of any single project and that a community indicator might decline even if a particular project is succeeding. One noted: "Water quality in a local stream may decline if upriver pollution offsets the success of our organization's programs to decrease toxic runoff." They worried that good work would be unrewarded because of circumstances out of an organization's control.

Others emphasized a different side of the problem:

> Focusing assessments on individual programs or projects can undermine the spirit of community collaboration needed to tackle big problems. It has a tendency to place too much attention on which organization gets credit for a given result. Project leaders can show how their work has ripple effects on larger community problems, but no one should take all the credit.

Comments like this one imply, usually without stating it directly, the need to link program accountability processes to collaborative community leadership mechanisms. If a small nonprofit program becomes part of a larger collaborative effort, it can receive credit for having done one piece of the needed work to achieve a community-level result. If improvements in one indicator are making one organization look good but creating unintended effects that plague other organizations—such as when a school achieves higher educational test scores by shunting large numbers of low-achieving students into alternative programs—a good collaborative can bring the issue to the table and negotiate change. If the community has been affected by

structural changes that make short-term improvements unlikely—
such as the closure of a timber mill—funders and community leaders
can keep results expectations reasonable across the board.

As Joan and I got in the car to leave after our final site visit, we
were still puzzling over what we had learned. A five-hour ride lay
ahead of us: a pretty drive that started off down Highway 101 through
the majestic redwoods of California's north coast, turned to cross the
wine grape–covered landscapes of Sonoma and Napa, and finally
landed us back in the flatlands surrounding Davis. During the ride,
learning that had been accumulating in slow increments suddenly
congealed. By the time we pulled into Davis, we had come up with a
way of explaining why the mētis-infused work of local nonprofits
could not be easily translated into the kind of accountability metrics
that mattered to their public and foundation funders (Campbell 2002).

The issue was scale. On the one hand, few specific projects have
sufficient scope to be held accountable for changing community-wide
indicators (e.g., the unemployment rate). On the other hand, the project-level outcomes for which they can be held accountable are typically so narrow that the public has no compelling accountability interest (e.g., training a dozen women in home business skills or
restoring an old ship in hopes of attracting tourists). Thus, leaders of
these nonprofit organizations faced a particular bind in responding
to the demands for results accountability. If they focused only on the
project-level outcomes over which they had the most control or for
which indicators were readily available, they risked default on the
larger question of accountability to publicly valued goals. But if they
tried to demonstrate the impact of their particular projects on community-wide outcomes, they risked taking credit inappropriately or
shouldering the blame for indicators beyond their control.

Outcomes assessment tools typically focus on either program performance indicators (United Way 1996) or measures of community
progress (Redefining Progress 1997), with comparatively little attention on how to build the linkages between these levels. This raises a
key accountability question: To what degree are particular projects
contributing to community-wide goals? A few pioneering efforts take
the difficulty of linking project-level and community-level outcomes
seriously (Friedman 2005; North Central Regional Center for Rural
Development 1997). These assume, however, that the community has

an agreed-upon process for overseeing the range of local development projects and charting future directions, a condition lacking in most locales (Bradshaw, King, and Wahlstrom 1999).

By the end of the Humboldt project, we had gained a more nuanced understanding of the scalar difficulties that appear in the space where metrics meets mētis. We had learned that the gap between the promise and practice of outcomes assessment is not simply a matter of inadequate training, slow learning curves, or deliberate evasion (Carter and Greer 1993), although all these factors sometimes play a role. The deeper reason is the presence of trade-offs that constrain even the best-trained and most willing of practitioners (Dicke and Ott 1999; Fredrickson 2000a), and the dependence of any results-based accountability system on working governance mechanisms and effective leadership.

Programs Are Embedded in Social Service Networks

The lessons we learned in Humboldt helped us bring a community network perspective to our later evaluation of the California Community and Faith-Based Initiative (Campbell 2011b; Campbell and Glunt 2006). At the time we conducted that evaluation, two issues dominated the research agenda on faith-based policy initiatives: (1) what role a "faith factor" played in how faith-related nonprofits delivered government-funded services (and thus whether faith-based initiatives could be conducted legally with respect to church-state constitutional guidelines) and (2) whether the services of faith-related organizations produced better results than those of government providers (Boddie and Cnaan 2006; Kennedy and Bielefeld 2006). Both framings presumed an evaluation approach that considered the funded organizations in isolation. Instead, as we learned in Humboldt and then from organizations like that of Veronica and George, the key issue was whether and how faith-related organizations could become valuable members of community service delivery networks.

Another example was provided by our encounter with Sally, a minister whose nonprofit organization links refugee populations to employment opportunities. Bilingual staff provide the bridge, identifying employers who can work around language and cultural barriers while coaching program participants one-on-one. For many reasons, her organization's participants often fear and distrust the government. A staff member states:

> Mostly our folks won't even enter the door of the government-run One-Stop. And if they do, they are not likely to feel at home. The One-Stop deals with everybody, whether you are low income or you're an executive of a company looking for a job, so there's a whole bunch of people walking in that door. But the way the performance standards are made, the One-Stop staff only want the people who are going to succeed. So a refugee walks in. Guess how many services they're going to get?

Sally's organization stepped into this breach to provide a wide range of culturally sensitive services. In essence, they became an alternative One-Stop, offering work-readiness assessments, résumé assistance, and active help with job placement and retention. Just like a One-Stop, they link their participants with compatible job opportunities while developing long-standing relationships with employers. Partner businesses become accustomed to welcoming refugees into their workforce. Meanwhile, Sally's nonprofit organization has become more attuned to employer needs so that the participants they refer are well prepared, cooperative, and high quality. All of the above depend on maintaining a position of trust and respect within the tight-knit Southeast Asian community, a relationship that requires ongoing nurturance and careful attention.

Interviews with refugees working with Sally's organization suggest that what matters is not so much the quality of any particular service they receive but how effectively the services they solicit from multiple community organizations aids their progress (Wuthnow 2004). "To get a job I needed a GED, and they helped me get connected with the adult school," said one. Another noted: "The events they sponsored helped me see a broader world than I see day-to-day. It gave me confidence that I might step out beyond my comfort zone." Other participants noted their disappointing experiences with other agencies, contrasting those with the welcome they received from Sally and her staff.

Over time, local workforce development officials came to recognize the important niche role Sally's organization played in the local network. They responded by offering to have two of her staff colocate at the One-Stop so that refugees walking in might have access to someone who speaks their language and understands their culture. These staff describe their experience at the One-Stop as stressful: "It's a large bureaucratic organization, very rigid, and feels very different from our home organization." Nevertheless, the new partnership succeeded in expanding access to workforce services among Hmong and other Southeast Asian populations.

The way community networks function calls into question an evaluation approach based on rigorous side-by-side comparisons of faith-based and secular programs (Campbell and Glunt 2006). Clients we interviewed testified that what most helped them was having one person they grew to trust who helped them navigate the local network and overcome difficulties. "The staff member helped me do everything I needed to do to get a job. I could not have figured out where to go or what to do without the help I received. I only wish they got me a job sooner."

Overall, our case studies of organizations like Sally's and Veronica and George's found that—once participants are in the door—they are better served by an approach that builds a well-functioning network of providers than they are by an implementation strategy that privileges a particular type of provider. Armed with the knowledge of the range of services provided by different organizations, network partners can knit together plans that draw on their respective strengths. With some imagination, they might also imagine ways to link this adaptive work to measurable indicators of network effectiveness, such as whether client referrals and other cooperative activities are handled effectively and efficiently. It was just such an approach that marked the effective youth services network that Maricela facilitated, as we learned in Chapter 1.

The Codetermination Work of Clients and Staff

Program-centric metrics necessarily narrow the frame of reference since to measure anything we have to isolate it from its surroundings.[2] But if we pay attention only to program metrics in developing public judgments, we will miss important dynamics that fall outside the sphere to which the metric attends. Having seen how program metrics can blind us to local network effects operating at the community scale, we now look in another direction. A partnership with colleague Lehn Benjamin led to critiquing the program-centric focus from a point of view focused on clients and frontline staff (Benjamin and Campbell 2015).

Consider what we learned in a workforce development program serving women in a small homeless shelter. Jaime, the sole staff person, was charged with linking the shelter residents with employment leading to stable housing. The state was interested in the employment and retention rate metrics of his homeless clients, but Jaime defined success in more immediate and tangible terms: getting someone to show up and stay engaged, seeing a depressed person smile, watching a client's self-esteem grow as they mastered working on a computer.

> I come to work, and the clients are waiting for me . . . happy or unhappy. Maybe they went to an interview and didn't get the job. So you've got to build their self-esteem. Maybe they need to apply for a different type of job, more suitable to them. Maybe they need to develop typing skills or computer skills so they are better prepared next time.

Jaime knew that he could not succeed without nurturing the self-worth of the women: "Being homeless, they have a lot of fears of dealing with society. So I have to convince them they are the same as anyone else. They happen to be in this situation, but they will come out of it." Jaime rejects any effort to categorize or stigmatize the homeless:

> I want to tell you right now that anybody can be homeless. You can be homeless in a matter of minutes if your boss says, "You're fired." We have a lot of families here who don't fit the stereotype, who are really smart but may have gotten into an accident or got divorced. Unfortunately, they have a bad name, but that's not the way I look at it.

He makes a point of not getting too close to his clients: "I need to keep some distance so I can push them when they need pushed. But also to protect my emotions . . . many of these women will fail." He knows that it is the clients themselves who ultimately have to act on their own behalf to succeed: "This one client was a drug addict for twenty-seven years. She didn't change because of me, I'll tell you that right now; she changed because she was ready. She kept saying it was me, but I go, 'No, it wasn't me; you changed because you were ready, and you were lucky enough to find me to help.'"

In an important sense, the sought-after employment results in this case depend on the relationship Jaime builds with his clients, not on any preset program of skill training or work readiness. Still, his state funders consider his effort a "program" and track metrics of whether the program's clients are gaining and retaining employment. Because they demand accountability for how he is using state funds, Jaime estimates he spends two or three hours of every eight-hour workday on state-required paperwork.

The blunt state metrics do not fit easily with the kind of work Jaime is doing. For one thing, many of those he serves are undocumented and thus never are formally enrolled or tracked by the state. "They do not have a birth certificate, a driver's license, a social security number . . . they come with nothing. So in order to get these clients ready to apply for jobs, or even to be considered formally enrolled in our program by the state, it can take six months or more to collect all the documentation." These clients draw on his time and effort while never showing up in state statistics.

When you ask the clients what about the program made the biggest difference in their experience, one hears story after story about Jaime going the extra mile on their behalf: finding just the right employment option after multiple failed attempts; calling clients on weekends so they would not miss out on a timely opportunity; simply being willing to spend time hearing out a client when they are feeling depressed. In summing up his role on the basis of our fieldwork, we used the phrase "routinely exceeds job description." Yet his effort, and many of his most treasured results, did not readily translate into official statistics.

During the years of fieldwork, I was again and again reminded of the practical power and deep commitment exhibited by so many of those working on the front lines of social policy. Evaluations or applied research that are focused on whether a particular program is producing results can miss the important point that it is often the choices of committed *people* and not *programs* that make the critical difference. Jaime is a good example. So are the welfare case workers we interviewed who made it *their* job to ensure low sanction rates rather than leaving it all up to the client. Everywhere we went there seemed to be one person who was dedicated to "cleaning up other people's messes," including the dysfunctions that occur where metrics and mētis collide.

Consider, as one more example, the story of an office secretary at a Merced County elementary school. Since the county's welfare school attendance project began, Alice's job had gotten a lot more difficult. The program's recordkeeping requirements were burdensome, well beyond just keeping track of whether students whose families received welfare were attending school. Now she had to track when they had accumulated a given number of unexcused absences, whether notification letters had been sent to parents, and if any of the mandatory parent conferences to discuss attendance problems (which she was responsible for scheduling) had been held. MerCAP implementation duties had been added on top of her already-full workday with no provision for extra support. She often worked weekends to complete the required paperwork, personally bearing the burden of a flawed program design that provided no new implementation resources. Alice had not been asked for advice before the program began, and she had little chance to influence the way the program was being implemented. In short, she had many good reasons to resent MerCAP as an unwelcome bureaucratic incursion.

But on meeting Alice, we saw not a trace of bitterness. As it turned out, she was strongly committed to the MerCAP goals, believing the program would encourage students to get to school and be better prepared for success later in life. The commitment sustained her through the long hours of recordkeeping. It also fortified her resolve to continue a role she had taken on before MerCAP began. At the beginning of every school day, after the teachers had reported which students were missing, she made it her business not just to call the students' homes but also to go get students who were home without good reason, picking them up in her personal car. She called it the "fun bus." The message to these students was clear: "You are important; we want you to succeed." Ironically, this was the same message MerCAP designers claimed they were trying to send, but the bureaucratic program they had packaged delivered another message entirely to welfare-receiving parents and their children: "You can't be trusted; we will punish you if you fail."

Evaluations typically overlooked important codetermination work shared by program participants and frontline staff. Far from simply receiving services and responding in programmatically intended ways, clients are active agents whose desires, attitudes, needs, and situational constraints play key roles in the change process (Keith-Lucas 1972). The organizations we studied found that permitting people to participate more actively in the conditions of their own care made good results more likely, including a result not often part of program metrics but of obvious value: increased dignity and self-respect (Sennett 2003).

Codetermination work poses dilemmas that necessitate mētis-informed, iterative judgments made amid considerable flux and uncertainty and in the context of ongoing pressures to document performance and client results. My colleague Lehn Benjamin and I describe how the highly individualized nature of codetermination work makes it inherently elusive. Yet in listening to the stories told by Jaime and others, we identified three essential elements: (1) establishing a relationship, (2) working out an agenda for change, and (3) taking action.

Establishing a Relationship

Drawing on skills like active listening and establishing rapport, staff seek to develop partnerships in which clients own the change process. As Jaime found, an initial issue is that clients are not equally ready to partner. They may lack crucial social skills, feel helpless, or suffer from depression or low self-esteem. Staff must respond with a wide variety of strategies to encourage clients to recognize their worth, capacity, and agency. For example, they provide small tasks that clients can pitch in to do, remind clients of their gifts, and ask clients to teach them things.

Most staff have been trained to maintain professional boundaries, but codetermination work forced them to step out of their professional expert role, or at least to hold that role with greater flexibility and humility. For example, one staff member explained she accepted gifts from clients even though this was seen as professionally inappropriate, because not to do so would be to suggest that she was somehow "above" her clients. Another states: "I might swear, you know, to show that equality. I'm just like you. I'm not any better."

This stance sets up a difficult balancing act, putting staff at odds with established organizational or professional norms, including the important need for clear boundaries to protect both themselves and clients from abuses: "I try to be as personable and as real as possible without being overly personable and overly real. And social workers kind of frown on that because people end up thinking you're their friend. But that's what this model calls for, so that we can communicate on a real level."

The skill with which staff navigate this dilemma has important consequences for outcomes. An immigration attorney told the story of a client who was reluctant to talk about her experience but who opened up after the two went to lunch and talked about their shared interest in cooking. The lunchtime rapport eventually helped the two build a better case for asylum.

Setting an Agenda

Determining what steps clients can and want to take and at what pace is a big part of codetermination work. Clients arrive with different resources, circumstances, and goals. While many programs include intake processes with elements of joint agenda setting, codetermination work involves honoring client autonomy, even when it runs at odds with program parameters. A common example in employment programs occurs when a client's articulated employment goals do not fit easily with established protocols. The program may be set up to secure entry-level jobs, but the client dreams of being a teacher or owning their own business. Staff must navigate this tension carefully, discerning whether and when to (1) let clients learn for themselves by testing the market; (2) reframe the client choice by honoring the motivation but helping them identify a series of short-term steps that get them moving toward their goal; or (3) provide a blunt reality check that may save the client from experiencing failure. Depending on the client, it may take considerable time to work through the options and arrive at a mutually agreed upon and effective course of action.

In the course of this work, staff struggle to know when to challenge clients and when to let go. Navigating this dilemma requires developing a feel for whether clients are ready to take risks by trying something new or letting go of something old, like encouraging a woman to leave an abusive relationship. For example, one caseworker described her work with domestic violence victims: "They need to do it when they are ready. No one can push them. If they are not ready, they will go back." Letting go can also simply reflect the realization that the broader conditions and circumstances affecting the client's life are overwhelming the benefits of any help.

How staff handle this dilemma has consequences for client outcomes. Not challenging adeptly can set someone up for failure, risk the relationship, or leave them stuck in circumstances that are detrimental. As one interviewee explains: "You have to know when to be a little bit pushy, and you have to know when to back off. That's a decision that you have to make every day. Because if you push when it's the wrong time, you're going to lose somebody. And if you back off when you should be pushing, then harm might come to them."

Taking Action

Ultimately, human services are about supporting client action to achieve new results for their lives. As one staff member noted, "When all is said and done, it's really up to them. We can support them, but unless they make a decision to change, their lives are not going to improve." This might involve something as simple as the client learning a new skill, more complex tasks such as figuring out how to clean up their credit history, or even bigger challenges like figuring out how to cope with mental illness or escape addiction. Considerable client apprehension often accompanies this dimension of codetermination work, particularly if there is a history of past failure.

Staff face a difficult discernment about when to (1) show clients what to do, because they do not know how; (2) do it for them, modeling the skill; (3) "walk with them" as they try something new, offering support; (4) refuse to assist so that a client will try on their own; or (5) do something on behalf of a client by advocating for them. These choices are shaped in varying degrees by formal organizational rules and program logics. For example, in one nonprofit there were rules that a client had to try something three times on their own before staff would assist. Yet language issues for non-English-speaking clients were often cited as justifications for "doing for" clients, at least in the short run. State mandates or regulations also can push staff to "do for." While the staff we interviewed offered several examples of how they discern their response, one in particular stood out. In a program that served victims of trauma and torture, victims seeking asylum have to go to court before a judge. Quite by accident, a staff member happened to observe a client hearing. The particular client found it so helpful to have a supportive person in the courtroom that it gave her the confidence she needed to testify effectively. Subsequently, staff sat in the courtroom on a regular basis, finding that being with clients as they testified produced better outcomes for their cases. The organization had previously discouraged staff from going with clients to avoid creating dependency.

Co-ownership of the change agenda typically increases participant motivation, supporting better results. This reality calls into question outcome measurement models that portray staff simply as program implementers and participants as merely recipients of services. Yet organizational leaders continue to face results accountability demands that make these assumptions.

Civic Time versus Programmatic Time

If they are to take seriously the insight that local network dynamics and client codetermination are important to achieving desired outcomes, the hidden heroes also need to address a third type of scalar conflict, this one involving time. Program-centric metrics organize community-supporting grantmaking into short bursts of time. In most of the evaluations I conducted, the intended outcomes were supposed to show up in two or three years, with grantee reports required yearly or more frequently. This is actually a comparatively long time in the grantmaking world. But it is still a fraction of what is actually needed to improve network effectiveness or observe significant change in the lives of burdened individuals.

A follow-up study (Campbell 2016) to our evaluation of the California Community and Faith-Based Initiative made it abundantly clear that the changes these organizations seek in client lives are complex and require action on multiple fronts over time. Clients may succeed in kicking their drug habit but fail to find employment. They may be on the road to recovery but be forced into housing choices that put them amid the same destructive influences that led them to drugs in the first place. They may succeed on all three fronts—sobriety, employment, and housing—for years, only to relapse under the stress of some difficult personal crisis.

If we broaden the lens to emphasize the community-scale and societal changes needed to better support these individuals, a long-haul perspective becomes even more essential. Community developers know that most meaningful changes to individuals or communities typically require chain reactions taking place over longer time spans (Harwood 2021; Kollock et al. 2012). In their own way, bureaucratic institutions provide for a continuity of focus on widely shared civic objectives over long spans of time. Yet, under the influence of neoliberal assumptions, our process for linking bureaucratic resources to community needs has adopted approaches and mentalities more consistent with the quarterly report mindset of the business world.

Meeting Grant Requirements versus Promoting Community Change

One of those quarterly report requirements became a flashpoint in an initiative our team evaluated (Campbell and Erbstein 2012). Devoted to "making communities better places for youth to grow up," this placemaking initiative was supported by a regional health foundation. We tend to associate foundation grantmaking with a freedom to experiment or take risks, and this is true in some ways. But in this case both parties to the grantmaking relationship described themselves as caught up in a bind not of their own making.

Foundation staff member Christine noted that they required the quarterly progress reports to satisfy a board made up of individuals from a business or government background: "Our board members have a pretty no-nonsense approach. They want to know the bottom line. We require grantees to report to us because we have a board that requires us to report to them. They take their fiduciary role very seriously." She portrayed herself as pinched on one side by her board and on the other by the wishes of grantees.

Adrianna, a community organizer and initiative grantee, described how the reporting requirement was taking time away from the community work they were being funded to do:

> We were reporting constantly. The quarterly progress reports took us a week to produce, and the time of numerous staff. It just seemed a little absurd. Most importantly, it didn't really sync with the way we work. We are constantly in an action-reflection cycle in our organizing work, and so we are making adjustments on the fly, including to our immediate goals and strategies. So following a blueprint we may have put into a grant proposal a couple of years earlier makes no sense in our world.

Adrianna's organization initially had pursued the youth development funding because they hoped to sponsor a youth conference in the neighborhood they were attempting to organize. But under the sway of the foundation's expectations for grantees, they quickly became caught up in a wide range of youth development activities. The funding relationship held great promise—putting foundation resources into one of the most economically distressed neighborhoods in the region. Ultimately, it led to some solid results, benefiting individual youth participants, altering the practices of some schools in response to student voice, and raising broader awareness of youth as community assets and citizens. But getting to these outcomes required each party in the grantmaking relationship to compromise on some of their normal ways of operating.

A key issue was time, in two senses. First, the community organizing group saw time as fluid and contingent. Its approach to developing leaders and pursuing policy change took for granted that not everything could be foreseen and planned in advance or achieved according to strict timelines. Adrianna notes: "We were willing to go along with the foundation's distinction between a planning phase and an implementation phase. But in reality we don't distinguish the two—organizing is a constant back-and-forth between planning and doing." By contrast, for the foundation time was organized, bounded, and controlled. Their initiative had clear start and end dates, with set amounts of funding available for certain lengths of time, so that the foundation budget could be managed.

Second, once grantees were selected the foundation felt some ownership over their time. They did not hesitate to make demands that grantees attend meetings at the foundation, without much regard for how this might affect grantees' ongoing work at the community level. For Adrianna, even the simplest and most taken for granted of foundation practices often grated:

> From the very beginning, they piled on meetings of all kinds. It was just overkill, like, "Here's another meeting to attend, another opportunity for you." But I'm like, "We have other work to do." It was overwhelming for me and for our youth participants. They even wanted us to cajole our community partners to attend some of the meetings, threatening the relationships we were building in the community.

Adrianna had a point. The initiative required her to attend meetings with foundation staff to review basic grant procedures and reporting requirements; meetings with the numerous technical assistance providers the foundation had hired; then additional meetings with a new set of technical assistance advisers when the foundation changed strategies midway through the grant; plus meetings with our evaluation team to provide feedback. And that's not to mention the various events to which grantees were expected to bring youth to participate. "We had a hard enough time getting youth to our own community meetings, and now we had this whole added set of expectations, which for youth meant complicated plans to arrange for transportation, parent communication, et cetera. It was all well intended, of course, and some of it turned out to be very useful."

From Adrianna's perspective, the foundation grant was just one set of resources to be deployed in ways that contributed to her organization's larger goal of organizing the community for change:

> I felt confused throughout the grant process about what was expected: youth development or policy change to support youth. Our goal is more the latter. If we can use the grant's resources and tools, great, but we're going to be here organizing for a long time. In some ways youth development is in conflict with our basic organizing model, which is built around long-

term personal and institutional relationships. And youth come and go.

With the foundation grant, a lot of youth service providers showed up just because there was money. Most of them have disappeared as the grant is coming to an end. It's the difference between a coalition model which the foundation was pushing and an organizing model the way we work. Sometimes the people the foundation expected us to bring to the table were the very people our organizing is trying to change.

Adrianna and her fellow organizers did stretch to accommodate the foundation's emphasis on engaging youth meaningfully. "With youth organizing, there are fewer one-on-one meetings, and youth have a different sense of time. Kids need to meet at a minimum every other week in order for a group or issue to maintain importance for them. What happened in those meetings created a space for youth of different backgrounds to work across ethnic boundaries, many for the first time."

Adrianna also acknowledged that the insistence of the foundation and technical assistance providers on honoring youth voice enabled their organization to develop new approaches. "We hired older youth as 'youth organizers,' offering them training but also giving them freedom to pursue ideas they felt committed to." Our evaluation team noted a case in point during the planning for a neighborhood youth conference. A planning team met to brainstorm issues that they felt would attract youth to the event. Two key topics they voiced were gangs and sex education: "Those are what will really get youth to attend." Adults in the planning meeting tried to steer the youth away from those topics, which they deemed too sensitive or controversial. But ultimately the youth prevailed, and the conference included well-attended presentations on both topics.

Christine reflected on some ways the foundation adjusted over the course of the grant while still insisting on certain terms of engagement:

> Normally if grantees are unhappy, we don't hear from them. With this initiative, we did hear a little grumbling about the number of meetings grantees had to attend and the amount of reporting. We learned that "more is not always more." We moved to semiannual reports rather than quarterly. And we

shifted the technical assistance to a model where providers went to grantees rather than asking the grantees to come to us.

Overall, we went out of our way to provide our grantees everything they needed to succeed. It was very important to us to make sure they all bought into our basic youth development framework and philosophy, so that we could be sure they were treating their youth participants in the right way. From past experience, we have learned that if we are not explicit, it doesn't happen.

Christine noted how distinct this initiative was from the foundation's normal grantmaking routines: "Usually, we are funding short-term grants, mostly one year. We just cut the check and don't hear from the grantee until we get the final report. This initiative was much more intensive from a workload perspective in order to promote the desired outcomes." She touted the fact that the initiative timeline, with grant support spread over three years, was the foundation's response to feedback from earlier grant recipients, who said one- or two-year grants were too short to make change happen. Of course the same might be said of a three-year initiative, especially one with the ambitious goal of changing local policies to better support youth. Indeed, one of Christine's colleagues we interviewed toward the end of the grant made a point of saying: "If we'd had five or six years, maybe we could have built more local capacity."

When Funders and Grantees "Meet Halfway"

The differences between programmatic time and civic time loomed large in the example just discussed, providing the backdrop to the frustrations of both parties to the grant relationship. Only by making concerted efforts to "meet halfway" were the parties able to persevere and produce a host of valuable outcomes for youth and their communities (Campbell and Erbstein 2012).

Foundations that are willing to adapt in response to grantee voices can support the kinds of evolutionary changes over time that produce the results that matter, not just the results as originally imagined.[3] In the Civic Engagement Project for Children and Families, the original focus of the funders on using deliberative dialogue encountered resistance from local civic engagement coordinators. They found that certain aspects of the dialogue model did not fit the diversity of people and community settings in which they were working. Neither did it fit with the ongoing evolution of local commissions, which had welcomed the dialogues as a way to spark initial planning but were looking for engagement strategies that better supported program implementation as the project moved into its second and third years.

After considerable discussion among the funder steering committee, the grantees were given the freedom to experiment with a broader range of civic engagement strategies. The shift did not come easily, and it resulted in the turnover of some of the steering committee and project staff. But the stance of responsiveness enabled the work to proceed in ways that supported a number of important outcomes, including fostering meaningful volunteer opportunities in schools, churches, neighborhood associations, parent groups, and national associations. In this fashion the three-year project built a legacy with the potential to improve the community over the long haul.

III

Lessons for Practice, Policy, and Theory

6

Redeeming the Promise of Results Accountability

A ssessment in various guises has become ubiquitous in contemporary life. We face the evaluative gaze as students, workers, managers, entrepreneurs, or even as volunteers. When we are the object of an evaluative assessment, we often have a rather cloudy sense of the how and why of the process. We may feel mistreated. We want to know, "How might my work, or the programs or organizations I am part of, be evaluated more fairly, taking into account a wide range of circumstances?" From a funder perspective, we might wonder, "How can our reporting requirements and evaluation processes enhance rather than detract from the pursuit of intended outcomes?" As policy analysts, we ask, "How might both funders and local implementers put their best foot forward, not to evade accountability but to learn from experience and from outcomes data?"

The case examples we have examined come from a particular niche of the policy world, focused on social services and workforce development programs. But the dynamics we have identified in that world—recurring dilemmas rooted in culture, rules, and scale—no doubt have similarities to those in many other evaluative assessment processes. The evidence we have gathered documents how these and related challenges routinely derail results accountability processes. At issue is whether understanding these failures can inform principles and practices that redeem the promise of results accountability as a tool of governance.

I begin this chapter by comparing results accountability processes that work well from those that work less well. I draw both on my own case evidence and on a few exemplary examples from other scholars and practitioners. The comparisons suggest three tentative principles to inform future policy and practice:

- Enhance emotional commitment and buy-in to the process
- Use fewer and more readily available metrics
- Encourage deliberative conversation because metrics do not speak for themselves.

I then offer four strategies for improving the work of evaluative assessment, drawing on the case evidence. These include

- Moving beyond program-centric myopia
- Locating deliberative processes inside institutions
- Rethinking grant reporting requirements
- Casting evaluators as facilitators of democratic learning

I close the chapter with broader reflections on the need to view results accountability not primarily as a set of techniques but as a demanding *practice* or *form* that encourages us to face reality head-on (Berry 1983; Levine 2015; MacIntyre 2007).

Why Results Accountability Regularly Fails and Sometimes Succeeds

Boiled to its essentials, results accountability requires three elements: (1) clarity in advance about a specifiable goal or goals being sought, (2) outcome measures that are readily available, reliable, and clearly linked to the goals, and (3) working feedback loops such that results data inform ongoing, goal-directed adaptations to policy and practice (Friedman 2005; Gardner 2005; Moynihan 2008; Radin 2006; Redefining Progress 1997; Wholey and Hatry 1992). Our fieldwork found that these elements are in short supply in ground-level practice.

TABLE 6.1. IMPEDIMENTS TO RESULTS ACCOUNTABILITY IN EIGHT COMMUNITY INITIATIVES*

Project	Goal clarity issues	Outcome data issues	Learning from results issues
Community Planning and Advisory Council	Multiple, very broad goals competed for attention	Sought quantification when it was not appropriate	Staff not skilled in facilitating deliberative conversation
Lassen Fitness Project	Goals clear but commitment from key players lagged	*Goals appropriately recast in less quantitative terms because of data feasibility/ availability*	Despite good results, the fiscal agent discontinued project
Civic Engagement Project	Experienced trade-off between participation and policy influence goals	Hard to derive indicators given broad goals and disparate activities	Funders more interested in lifting up success stories than confronting limitations
REACH Youth Development	Youth development and policy change goals competed	No common indicators to track given differences in settings and approaches	Tendency of grantees to cling to initial work plans too long
Merced County Attendance Project	Faulty premise; state and local agency goals did not align	Attendance data not uniformly collected and thus costly to obtain/analyze	Results data ignored by local leaders who resisted needed adjustments
Community and Faith-Based Initiative	Workforce goals competed with existing nonprofit priorities	Mandated performance measures ignored key intermediate outcomes	*EDD staff provided good feedback loop between grantees and state agency*
Workforce Investment Act	Social service and economic development goals diverged	Mandated performance measures led to gaming numbers and "creaming"	Distrust impeded needed deliberation and ongoing adaptation
Workforce Investment Act Youth Programs	Tension between goal of immediate employment and training for the long term	Data management and reporting system out-of-date	Local lessons did not influence changes to federal and state policy

* The two cells in *italics* represent successful adaptations rather than impediments.

Across eight major evaluations my teams conducted, there was not a single case in which all three elements aligned.

To reach this conclusion, I constructed a twenty-four-cell table in which each cell contained a summary indication of whether one of the three criteria had been met by each project (see Table 6.1). Drawing on our evaluation reports, I was deliberately scanning for counterindications of a significant nature, not minor setbacks. Sadly, such evidence was remarkably easy to identify. Of the twenty-four cells, there were only two (indicated by italics) in which results accountability criteria had been satisfied without significant complications or qualification.

Each of the eight projects struggled to realize any one of the three requisite conditions, yet the results accountability model presumes that all three are aligned. We discovered again and again what is familiar to anyone who has tried to develop a working results accountability scheme: the work calls for a degree of clarity about purposes that is rare, raises thorny questions of data availability and quality, and forces persistent trade-offs between what would be ideal and what is feasible. Our findings are consistent with previous studies emphasizing the limits of outcomes assessment strategies as an aid to everyday governance and policy practice (Bass and Lemmon 1998; Carter and Greer 1993; Cobb and Rixford 1998; Dicke and Ott 1999; Hart 1999; Newcomer 1997; Saidel 1991; Sawicki and Flynn 1996).

In light of the accumulating evidence, we need to practice results accountability with a mixture of boldness and humility—reaching for the ideal without expecting that it can be easily routinized. Our fieldwork provided a deeper and more sympathetic understanding of the difficulties surrounding its use. As described in the next section, we first learned this in projects in Lassen and Humboldt Counties, where our efforts to teach outcomes assessment techniques encountered numerous obstacles.

The Grip of Scientism and the Central Role of Relationships

Located in the mountains and high desert of northeastern California, Lassen County is among the largest California counties in area (4,547 square miles) but one of the smallest in population (around 34,000).

Susanville is the only incorporated city, and as the county seat it provides the majority of the public services. Lassen County residents who live in the outlying areas have difficulty accessing these services because of the rugged terrain and the lack of public transportation.

We went to Lassen to provide technical assistance and evaluation services to a grant-created nonprofit, the Community Planning and Advisory Council (ComPAC). In response to the California Endowment's call for proposals, ComPAC leaders had committed to incorporating the new nonprofit organization, identifying indicators of a "healthy community," and launching projects to improve those indicators. ComPAC leaders chose to embrace a broadly defined set of initiatives to promote economic opportunities, strong families, quality education, holistic health, environmental protection, and civic infrastructure.

The sweeping goals left them with a dizzying array of potentially applicable outcome metrics. Further, there was confusion about how broad or narrow the indicators should be, reflecting a lack of clarity about how to differentiate program indicators, ComPAC organizational indicators, and community-wide indicators. As the difficulties mounted, anxiety grew among leaders and participants.

We found that project staff burdened themselves with a perceived standard of scientific validity that was out of proportion to their situation and resources. They tended to seize on any opportunity to gather quantifiable data, without thinking much about its value, cost, or feasibility. Meanwhile, community members found the effort to identify outcome indicators abstract and confusing, preferring concrete action projects, which elicited greater community enthusiasm and participation.

Ironically, the difficulties over results accountability expectations became most pronounced with the activity participants identified as the most successful ComPAC endeavor. The organization funded a series of mini-grants ($500–$3,000) sprinkled among private citizens and nonprofit groups, supporting short-term activities like beautification projects on Main Street, antismoking projects in local schools, and brochures to attract movie production to the county. ComPAC leaders attempted to hold these grantees accountable for reporting quantifiable outcomes, hoping this would help them document outcomes for the funder. In leading a training for mini-grant recipients, we suggested a different approach that emphasized modest but reasonable quantitative data along with narratives of public impact. Project leaders took offense, believing we were not doing what they had hired us to do or what their expectations of university experts had led them to believe we would do.

In Humboldt we also observed the strong grip of the culture of "scientism." We initially presumed that leaders of nonprofit economic development organizations could identify outcome indicators linking their project work to commonly valued community-level outcomes. But even though project developers were acutely aware that their grant funding did not pay enough to support rigorous evaluation or data development, they put pressure on themselves to meet the highest standards of evidence. Our role as university-based researchers exacerbated the issue—the local leaders assumed that our bar would be set very high. As time went on and their search for indicators floundered, we realized we had to be explicit in encouraging them to expand the types of evidence that might serve as valid outcome indicators. For example, if the outcome was "increased awareness and information about business opportunities," it was feasible and practical to use participant self-reports as an indicator rather than requiring a more sophisticated pre- and post-test survey.

Identifying community-level outcomes posed a different set of difficulties for the Humboldt leaders. By their very nature, community goals are subject to multiple interpretations and ongoing negotiation. This has been especially true in the volatile setting of timber-related communities like Humboldt as they deal with perceived conflicts between the environment and jobs. When we asked nonprofit project developers whether they would feel comfortable linking their projects to community-wide goals, the immediate response was often, "Who gets to set the goals? Who gets to say what is important?" They were wary of any attempt to force projects to conform to an "official" list of priorities, believing it would risk eliminating important projects that did not fit the current or dominant agenda.

Asked to rate fifty-one potential economic development indicators, the Humboldt area funders we surveyed frequently appended qualifications to their ratings, expressing acute awareness of the limits of data availability and quality, suggesting nuances that made determining the meaning of any given indicator difficult, or offering local exceptions and circumstances that colored seemingly unambiguous figures. They seemed to share the judgment of many experts that although indicators are presented quantitatively, they remain interpretations of reality in the same way that words are narrative interpretations of reality (Cobb and Rixford 1998, 14; Fredrickson 2000b, 8; Murphey 1999).

The primary benefit to be gained from outcomes assessment metrics is in establishing agreed-upon standards, with the goal of limiting bias in measuring performance. Yet both nonprofit leaders and their funders in Humboldt said that developing trusting personal relationships was typically a more valuable investment of time and energy than collecting or analyzing outcome data. One project developer stated, "It's the people connected to the project that are its best assets, and the success of the project is tied to their personal energy. Indicators are fine, but there shouldn't be a direct link between them and funding."

When Results Accountability Succeeds

It is instructive to examine successful examples of the use of results accountability, comparing them with the failures and limitations we observed across our suite of evaluation and technical assistance projects. Let us consider four examples, the first from my own work and three from other sources.

The Lassen Fitness Project
A project to promote community fitness in Lassen County provides the first example, offering an instructive contrast to the ComPAC experience just discussed.[1] The goal of the fitness project was to promote community wellness by increasing the physical activity levels of Lassen County residents. In meeting this goal, project leaders confronted built-in obstacles: harsh winters, limited access to indoor recreational facilities, and a public culture that paid little attention to the desirability of physical fitness. Two very capable and civically engaged project codirectors guided the work, part of their affiliation with a community outreach unit of the local hospital. The hospital had received the grant from the James Irvine Foundation as part of a statewide program to promote community health and civic investment.

One key to the project's success was that the two leaders adapted their approach to results accountability to fit the situation at hand. Their grant proposal had articulated project goals in the rigorous terms they assumed would appeal to the foundation, promising (1) to increase by 25 percent the community's knowledge of the benefits of regular physical activity and exercise; (2) for individuals participating through project partners (i.e., physicians, workplaces, and faith communities) to increase by at least 15 percent their participation in regular physical activity or exercise to at least five times per week; (3) to increase by 20 percent from year one to year two area businesses' involvement as partners in a community-wide fitness project; and (4) to investigate the efficacy and effectiveness of a community-wide fitness project on individual and community health status.

During our original consultation with project leaders, we noted that the objectives themselves appeared quite sound but that the effort to rigorously quantify three of the objectives was not likely to prove useful given the available time and resources.[2] Project leaders took the advice to heart, opting to gather a wide range of outcome evidence, including both quantitative data and narrative descriptions. Their marriage of metrics and mētis did not meet the high benchmarking standards suggested by their original grant proposal. However, as the following excerpts from the final evaluation report demonstrate, they sufficed to give a rich flavor of the work and to document its public value:

Get Up and Get Moving. In this program, physician partners (including physical therapists and chiropractors) referred clients to the Fitness Project. A letter was sent to more than 20 area health care providers and about 50% were signed up to participate by making referrals. Participation in the program grew from 13 referrals in April 1998, to 87 in October 1998, to 150 in February 1999. Those referred receive a packet of materials with a wide range of practical information on starting a personal fitness program and a phone call from a Fitness Project leader. The materials covered a variety of substantive topics in a professional yet friendly and accessible manner. The general philosophy is expressed in the program's title: just get going—in other words, anybody can do this. A survey of program participants was conducted periodically, and suggests the program was highly successful in encouraging regular physical exercise. Of the 43 respondents, 17 reported exercising five or more days per week and 37 reported exercising at least 3 days per week. A large majority (36 of 43) reported positive changes in their health since starting the exercise program. Open-ended comments reported high satisfaction.

Community Media. Project leaders used a variety of media to reach the community with practical fitness information. These included paid radio ads three times a week, radio Public Service Announcements three times a week, a monthly "fitness person" profile featured in the weekly newspaper, the *Healthy Lassen Newsletter*, and a "Get Up and Get Moving Directory" that listed local places to go and things to do to be physically active. Each month there was a special "Fitness Theme" such as cardiovascular fitness, flexibility, family exercise, or strength training. Our post-project interviews suggested that these activities were successful in gaining the attention of many community residents. Most people to whom we mentioned the Lassen Fitness Project recognized the name and associated it—very positively—with inserts in the paper, T-shirts they had seen around town, and a variety of health and fitness programs they had heard of or experienced. As one community member put it: "There was a lot of good feeling in the community about that project—people used to talk about it with pride."

Note how both of these narrative summaries blend activity descriptions, outcome evidence, and considerations of local context. This provided a more meaningful and less intrusive (for participants) way to report on project outcomes than would have been the case in attempting to generate more precise pre-post measurements.

Teen Pregnancy in Tillamook County

A second example comes from a story told by one of the most thoughtful experts on results accountability, Mark Friedman. He recounts how Tillamook County, Oregon, was able to lower its teen pregnancy rate from one of the highest among Oregon counties to the lowest

(Friedman 2005, 36–38). A published metric in a 1990 state report had shocked residents into recognition that they had a problem. Community pride took a blow. Having recently rejected a proposal to put health clinics in high schools, residents of the socially conservative county faced the issue of how else to address their teen pregnancy problem.

A wide range of potential solutions surfaced, not all of them compatible with one another. We might have expected a polarized debate with different sides marshaling experts to support their preferred alternative, the "one best way" to tackle the problem. Instead, community leaders built a diverse coalition in which everyone was invited to do what they thought was best. By casting one another as partners working toward a shared civic goal rather than as combatants debating the best approach, the community activated itself. Schools altered their curriculum to emphasize self-esteem and sex education. Churches taught refusal skills and abstinence. The County Health Department expanded clinic hours and reduced wait times. The YMCA provided recreation activities. The community college worked with student parents to prevent second unintended pregnancies. The combined effect of the community efforts showed clear results: the teen pregnancy rate declined for four consecutive years at a time when the overall rate in Oregon remained flat.

We can imagine other ways this scenario might have played out. Someone in authority might have insisted that letting multiple change strategies proliferate would not help to determine which ones were working or not working. In search of evidence-based policy, he or she might have insisted on comparative program evaluations so that resources could be targeted to programs that succeeded. But all that evaluation would have required data collection, imposing substantial costs in terms of time and resources. It would have diverted the attention of the on-the-ground implementers from doing the activities they had chosen and focused it instead on providing evidence that their approach was working.

A few elements of this story stand out. First, the issue commanded the attention of a wide range of actors for a significant period of time, something rare in politics (Stone, Orr, and Worgs 2006).[3] Second, the multiplicity of strategies deployed meant that weaknesses in any one approach were less important in derailing the overall process. We can imagine that the collective success brought forth a certain civic humility, as everyone recognized the dependence of success on others. Third, the catalyzing metric—based on data the state routinely collected—played a pivotal role without draining resources from the local activities that were making a difference. Finally and perhaps most tellingly, no external entity was holding the community accountable for achieving a result. The work was motivated by the community itself, for its own reasons and using its available resources. The citizens of Tillamook could say, with conviction, "We did it, and our doing it made a difference."

PerformanceStat

A third example is the PerformanceStat/CitiStat model as popularized by Robert Behn (2014) and now used in dozens of U.S. cities. At one level, the model is straightforward. City leaders convene regular accountability meetings that hold frontline managers to performance targets while enabling greater deliberation and flexibility in how targets are achieved. The meetings are routine and recurring and always involve the presentation of charts, graphs, and other data depicting trends and identifying hot spots needing attention. Subsequently, there is an opportunity to reflect on the data from multiple perspectives, always grounded by a shared goal, such as reducing crime in a neighborhood. The meetings provide a space to negotiate mutual and collective accountability among partners at the community level rather than a process that looks for scapegoats or limits itself to issues of vertical accountability for fairness and finances.

Behn digs deeper, however, in searching for explanations for why this model works as well as it does.[4] He finds that the key is how leaders actively link "explicit knowledge about 'What?'" to "tacit knowledge about 'How?'" (2014, 246–247). In his view, results accountability is the product not of a mechanistic system but of a leadership strategy:

> Thus, the challenge facing the leadership team is not to build some new, fabulous machine. Rather it is to work with the existing people, relationships, and structures—injecting some conscious purposes, creating some specific targets, inspiring

with public recognition, devoting time while remaining persistent . . . all the while analyzing data, asking questions, scrutinizing reports, in an effort to learn whether their leadership behaviors are introducing new feedback loops that foster adaptations that help to achieve the purposes. (254)

In this description, we find all the elements of a working results accountability process: goals, data, and deliberation. We also find a vivid description of how local leadership is needed to realize a working results accountability scheme.

After-Action Review

A final example comes from the military, in some ways a prototypical bureaucracy but one that also depends on the mētis-infused wisdom of its troops. When Canadian military troops deployed to Afghanistan, they had clear rules of engagement. But they also were specifically trained that in the moment, as they made frontline, often life-or-death decisions, they were free to ignore these rules, provided they could justify their actions later. "Later" was a recurring institutional practice called an "after-action review" where all the members of a deployed team gathered to debrief the mission. For cases in which a team member or members had worked around the operative rules of engagement, each member explained what they did and why. The purpose was to learn as an organization, refining the rules of engagement to be more closely aligned with on-the-ground realities. Presumably, incorporating the learning into subsequent trainings would reduce casualty metrics when later teams deployed.

Military hierarchy and discipline did not go away in the review setting, but it was mediated in important respects. The flexible nature of the initial orders gave soldiers permission to use discretion. That stance created an expectation that the organization was committed to learning. The team meeting provided certain check on reporting that ventured too far from reality; it was not a perfect check, but if something were to be hidden, a relatively large number of individuals would have to do so in a face-to-face setting. Finally, the life and death reality of war provided the underlying urgency: "People like me or people I know could be killed if we don't get this right."

Emerging Principles

I introduced the comparisons in this section by noting that results accountability processes require an alignment among (1) goal clarity, (2) data availability, and (3) working feedback loops. The case examples show how difficult it can be to achieve any one of these three elements, much less their alignment. But they also suggest three tentative principles to consider if we want results accountability process to work better.

First, emotional buy-in and commitment matter. Where there is a strongly felt sense of urgency, a sense that lives are at stake or that something vital needs to be preserved, it is more likely that goals will be clear and firmly held. We saw examples of this in the Tillamook story and the after-action reviews of the Canadian military. In a less dramatic fashion, we saw it in the laser focus of the Lassen Fitness Project leaders on improving the health habits of community members. By contrast, if outcome reporting is viewed solely as a way to appease superiors or funders, as was the case with ComPAC leaders, it will be more difficult to maintain clarity over time and sustain initial commitments. The type of focus I have in mind is suggested in the phrase "this cannot stand," a sentiment that has catalyzed many effective policy initiatives.[5]

Second, results accountability works well when outcome metrics are relatively few in number and use regularly collected statistical data. Of note, this is the case in bureaucratic agencies or their subunits that have a singular focus and charge. By contrast, in many community-supporting grant processes—particularly those sponsored by foundations—the goals are broadly cast. Local implementers are charged with determining or collecting outcome and indicator data themselves, a process that can be confusing or difficult and that takes time away from the work of creating outcomes.

However well-intended or backed by impressive theories of change, comprehensive community change initiatives often make it extraordinarily hard to align goals with data; there are simply too many variables or potential data points with which to contend. The confusion ComPAC leaders encountered in trying to work on a broad suite of healthy community goals and indicators is a case in point. The recommendation that grantees develop logic models can exacerbate the difficulties. To be sure, logic models can be helpful in assisting grantees to organize around shared goals and to think through the connections between their actions and intended outcomes. On the other hand, they tend to generate long lists of outputs and outcomes to be tracked or measured. This tracking and measuring work can be confusing or tedious, draining energy from the work itself.

Finally, metrics cannot speak for themselves. They require deliberative conversation to interpret their meanings and implications. Overall, funders should put less emphasis on gathering extensive data and more on promoting deliberation. On a practical level, this requires creating, defending, and staffing institutional spaces and routine organizational practices in which learning and deliberation are the primary ends. It also requires moving beyond the program-centric myopia that characterizes most evaluative processes.

Building on these emergent principles, the next four sections offer strategies that might improve policy and practice.

Moving beyond Program-centric Myopia

Results reporting typically is couched in a relatively narrow frame of reference, bound to a specific period of time and to grant-funded programs considered in isolation. As our examples have shown, this narrowing makes sense from the perspective of the central authorities who need to monitor how their funds are being used and what outcomes can be attributed to particular grant interventions. But the narrow lens makes less sense if our concern is with the overall functioning of a community social service system, the ability of human services clients to sustain personal change, the capacity of citizens to engage in public work, or the manner in which a single grant contributes or detracts from preexisting community change trajectories.

My own early experience in Cooperative Extension, as a funder of local food system initiatives, provided an eye-opening lesson along these lines. As a staff member at the University of California Sustainable Agriculture Research and Education Program (UC SAREP), I worked with my colleague Gail Feenstra to manage a competitive grant program. Gail and I conducted a case study of a local success story as part of an effort to document the outcomes of that program.

We chose to focus on PlacerGROWN, a local agricultural marketing organization (Campbell and Feenstra 2001, 2005). Our report showcased an impressive list of PlacerGROWN activities and achievements. However, local leaders had struggled to produce community-scale outcome metrics as encouraged by our grant. When we called this shortcoming out in a draft case study report, I received a strong rebuke from a local extension colleague. We were not wrong, she said, but more than a little tone deaf.

Our difference was a matter of perspective. As funders, we were looking at PlacerGROWN as a single project among our suite of university-funded projects. Our interest was relatively narrow and focused entirely on the time frame of our grant: What had our investment of university funds generated in terms of results that mattered at the community scale? This was the type of information we needed to satisfy university bureaucrats skeptical of our program. What the local colleague's response helped us understand was the importance of taking a longer and more locally relevant time frame into account. The most important impact of PlacerGROWN, from her point of view, was the continuity it provided with past organizing efforts in the community, including the creation of farmers' markets in the late 1980s, as well as the impetus it was giving to new initiatives moving forward.

Like many funders, we hoped to document a grantmaking success. But by narrowing our sights to the immediate grant, we were missing key parts of the larger context of meaning in which the work was unfolding. As I would experience later in evaluating other complex community change initiatives, this kind of myopia on the part of funders is all too typical. By subsequently stepping back to consider the bigger picture, Gail and I adjusted in a way that supported new learning while repairing the relationship with our colleague. We emerged with a better appreciation of the time it takes to make community change and of how the concrete work we had funded fit into a broader history of community initiative.

How might assessment and evaluation processes be rethought to move beyond program-centric myopia? The hidden hero stories point to approaches funders and program implementers might consider. Building on the evidence in Chapter 5, these approaches address the challenges posed by client codetermination, network dynamics, and civic time.

Taking Client Codetermination into Account

Appreciating the role of client codetermination in supporting results suggests an approach particularly applicable in human services.[6] Co-ownership of the change agenda by staff and clients typically increases participant motivation, supporting better outcomes. This reality calls into question outcome measurement models that portray staff simply as program implementers and participants as merely recipients of services. How might we respond?

First, we need to value client-defined, short-term outcomes that may be different from those articulated in program logics. It is clear that not all clients will choose to take the same paths toward achieving longer-term goals. It is those microlevel variations that can make the difference between client success and failure and that get missed by preset performance models and their metrics.

Second, codetermination work has its own outcomes. The effectiveness of staff in supporting codetermination work and resolving key dilemmas shapes whether a client develops a greater sense of their own agency or remains dependent. Importantly, this enhanced sense of agency (which itself could be measured) can be transferred to a range of client issues and problems beyond those specified by a particular program intervention.

Third, codetermination work supports the sustainability of client outcomes. If the work is poorly done, such as by pushing a client too quickly or forcefully toward actions that they do not own, client outcomes are less likely to be sustainable.

Finally, by expanding democratic capacities, codetermination work can link the particular outcomes of human services nonprofits to the broader nonprofit sector goal of advancing the civic agency of marginalized communities and individuals. The secret is in deploying strategies that repair confidence, self-esteem, and hope and, with those, the sense of one's capacity to act.

Linking Grantmaking to Community Governance Mechanisms

Our work in economic and workforce development suggests a different approach to results accountability that relies on effective community governance mechanisms. In one scenario funders of projects in a particular community coordinate their efforts to focus on a discrete set of outcomes, provide grantees with the assistance needed to develop valid and useful indicators—for example, by centrally funding key data development activities—and then actually use the results to determine future funding decisions (Gardner 2005). A second scenario would require local project collaborators to argue their way to a consensus on selected goals, figure out which organizations and projects can contribute, and then reach out collectively to a funder or funders for both project resources and support for data development. Based on our Humboldt experience, neither scenario is achievable without serious focus and effort supported by effective community leadership.

Mark Friedman has developed two particularly useful recommendations to guide communities who want to link program- or project-level work to community-scale outcomes. The first is to have a regular report card tracking key indicators so that progress and regress can be monitored. The second recommendation he calls "Turning the Curve." This involves regularly convened forums where people can meet, assess progress, and take action (Friedman 2005, 17–38).

The latter process is intended to move a community from talk to action in a relatively short period of time. First, a key indicator is located, and trends related to this indicator are examined to determine the severity of a problem. Then metrics meet mētis creatively, as participants are encouraged to articulate "the story behind the baseline," using their combined experience to flesh out a tentative and context-specific answer to the question "What is going on?" Next, they brainstorm how to enlist different individuals or organizations that have resources to bring to bear on the problem. An action plan results, with the goal of "turning the curve" on the problem by taking a bad trend and moving it in the desired direction (or accelerating a positive trend). Ideally, the process then repeats itself at regular intervals.

View Individual Projects in a Longer-Term Trajectory of Community Change

A third approach would address funders directly, urging them to make a concerted effort to consider any single grant project or initiative within a long-term trajectory of community change. To do this, grant reports would be need to become occasions for sharing not just short-term, project-specific outcome metrics but also differing perspectives on their meaning and implications, informing debates about what needs to happen next (Newfield, Alexandrova, and John 2022, 2). These conversations would deliberately take into account a wide range of public values and community dynamics and reference a longer time horizon. They would attempt, however imperfectly, to speak across the cultural and scalar divides between center and periphery.

Locating Deliberative Processes inside Institutions

Repeatedly, our research found results accountability processes breaking down at the point where some form of deliberative conversation was needed but missing. Our evidence echoes the academic literature on results accountability: a key observed flaw is the failure to close the loop by ensuring that outcome data are used to spark dialogue about appropriate adjustments to future policy and programs (Behn 2001; Moynihan 2008; Radin 2006). Put simply, we appear to be generating far more data than conversation, more reports than inquisitive readers. In this environment, information accumulates like noise, and facts can be found to justify any point of view. But meaningful discussions of the meaning and implications of data are in short supply.

During the decades in which we were witnessing these difficulties in closing the loop, a movement to promote deliberative democracy was developing on a parallel track. That movement shares with results accountability the goal of figuring out "the right way to do the right thing" (Schwartz and Sharpe 2010). While many of the preferred methods touted by deliberative democrats promote active listening, they typically do so in artificially created settings that remain distant from real-world decision-making processes. Instead, we need to find ways to insert deliberative conversation closer to the center of those processes.

A good evaluation report can invite a dialogue by juxtaposing the reflections of the many different partners to a project, including participants. But there is no guarantee that the reports will be read by the right people or used for continuous learning, bringing diverse perspectives into conversation with one another. In our own practice as evaluators committed to fostering learning communities, we typically lacked the time, focus, committed partners, and sustained intentionality to make these conversations come into being. For example, in the workforce system evaluation, workaround stories pointed to implementation flaws needing correction, but state and local officials seldom came together to deliberate what those corrections might entail. Nor did we take active steps to initiate such a conversation, although our reports did point out the need for one. In retrospect, this was a missed opportunity.

In government programs the sheer volume of reporting can crowd out space for deliberation. Deliberation takes time, and time is at a premium in most institutional settings. As Karpowitz and Mansbridge (2005) and Lee (2007) have argued, many deliberative processes fail precisely at this point. They are constrained by time frames that are not sufficient to find and forge consensus on how policy and programs might be adjusted on the basis of outcome data. In meeting our own reporting deadlines as evaluators, we felt the rush to get things done just as much as the grantees did. Like them, we breathed a sigh of relief when our final report was submitted and we could move on to other projects. Funders also need to move on to the next grant process. In this way, the relentless grind of relatively short-term program cycles builds in a bias against the deliberative conversations that need to happen. For foundations, it also can preclude "rolling up" lessons learned from across a suite of local projects with similar objectives.

Steps in the Right Direction

The elusive goal is to reduce nonessential paperwork and compliance demands, thus freeing time for more substantive reflection on data and experience. Most human service delivery institutions would benefit from an ongoing review of the system's audit and compliance functions. A key feature of this review would be the active engagement of local representatives and frontline staff, joining their voice to those of state and federal officials to determine how accountability processes can be streamlined while still providing appropriate checks and balances.

Workaround stories hold some promise in promoting such learning. By clustering and aggregating these stories, we can better discern common flaws in policy design, difficulties with certain implementation procedures, and the managerial dispositions that create space for creative local adaptation (Campbell 2012). Similar approaches have guided reform efforts in fields as diverse as information systems (Azad and King 2008), ergonomics (Courtright et al. 1988), health care (Johnson, Miller, and Horowitz 2008), nursing (Vestal 2008), and warfare (Ambrose 1997).

The need for deliberation to "move inside" is just as necessary in foundation grant processes as it is in government. As we saw in the case of Adrianna's organization and her foundation funder, nonprofit leaders often find themselves in an awkward position vis-à-vis the deliberative goals of results accountability. Grantees need foundation funds, but the short-term outcome measures that grants require seldom comport perfectly with a nonprofit's long-term organizational mission or change strategy. Rather than confront this discrepancy head-on in deliberative conversation with their funders, there is a tendency to treat the reporting requirements as a necessary chore to be completed with a minimum of reflection rather than risk their relationship by entering a more thoughtful, if sometimes difficult, conversation.

Foundation funders too can avoid a true reckoning, preferring to look for signs their initiatives have succeeded rather than digging into a balanced assessment of what worked, what did not, and why. The small, sometimes grudging steps Adrianna and Christine took toward meeting halfway are the types of practical accommodation that begin to move partners beyond their built-in differences of perspective.

Integrated Services Teams as a Container for Deliberation

The work of local integrated service teams provides one model of what moving deliberation inside institutions can achieve. These cross-agency teams come together regularly (weekly, biweekly, monthly, etc.) to share resources, capitalize on their diverse assets, and strategize over how to overcome bureaucratic obstacles. The regularity of the meetings allows time and space to focus on both metrics and practical, actionable remedies, not just on getting the numbers right but deliberating on their meaning and implications.

In interviews, individuals working in these integrated services partnerships exuded a strong sense of individual and collective agency, made possible by a movement from isolation to a greater sense of teamwork in the pursuit of shared civic objectives. Examples we witnessed included staff from different agencies debating how to better coordinate childcare services among clients they share in common; representatives of community colleges, workforce boards, and welfare agencies devising a new welfare-to-work pathway that works for clients and their own organizations; and fiscal officers wrestling with how funds can be better mingled in joint projects while still meeting the audit requirements of their individual agencies.

Service integration is, by its nature, an insider's game, a sort of gated community with restricted access. As I came to admire the work of these teams, I wondered why their achievements are mostly invisible to the public, who could use a dose of their encouraging stories to counter the negative public perception of public servants. It is also true that the insiders would benefit from perspectives not included at their meeting tables, especially those of the program participants, families, and neighborhoods they seek to serve. In interpreting community-level data and trends, it would be quite beneficial to balance the insights of system insiders with the voices of community residents, creating a broader tapestry within which to examine causes and effects or to debate alternatives.

Daniela's struggles to promote civic engagement among parents of young children (Chapter 3) showed just how difficult it can be to insert lesser-heard voices into the insider-centered tables of the policy world, even at the local level. The effort to broaden the community of those influencing policy met up against the reality that any particular deliberative tool has both strengths and weaknesses. Commission-appointed advisory committees had more influence on substantive decisions but tended to elicit the participation of established experts and insiders. By contrast, well-facilitated community forums or conversations created nonthreatening spaces for hearing from a wide range of parents, but this came at the cost of working through conflicts to arrive at a strong consensus view to present to decision-makers.

Taking Emotions into Account

One of the less heralded but important obstacles to the needed deliberative conversations is the rational veneer that results accountability and democratic deliberation both present, which tends to blind their proponents to the important role of emotions in public life (Forester 1999). As Ivan Illich argues, in exercising agency humans are often moved "in the gut."[7] Yet emotions do not seem to have a home amid the logic models and the careful, rational weighing of pros and cons that anchor many results accountability processes.

Attending to emotions can aid the process of deliberation by helping us identify where problems are most acutely felt and alerting us when a particular solution is resonating with its intended beneficiaries (Peters, Alter, and Shaffer 2010). In this sense, eliciting and learning from emotional responses is an important result in its own right. It may be a particularly important point of entry as we attempt to wed metrics and mētis more productively.

In Tillamook, wounded community pride catalyzed positive civic action. But pride can also get in the way of deliberation that moves policy in the right direction, as we learned during our evaluation of the Merced County Attendance Project (MerCAP). The ample state funding our team received enabled us to design a rigorous evaluation featuring quantitative analysis of administrative data on school attendance and also a detailed process analysis of the program's implementation. Contrary to the program's basic premise, we found that the pre- and postproject attendance of welfare students was nearly identical to that of nonwelfare students. Indeed, attendance for both groups was quite high, in the range of 95–96 percent (Campbell and Wright 2005). Further, our interviews and focus groups made it clear that health issues were the primary driver of absences, such that an intervention providing better health care would be more likely to achieve the program's goal, for *all* students.[8]

Our state-required quarterly evaluation reports, distributed to Merced Human Service Department leaders, shared these findings. They also reminded local implementers that the state waiver they were operating under included specific instructions that sanctions were to be used only as a last resort after case management interventions were tried. Instead, the implementation never included a significant case management effort, while sanctions were routinely employed. Program developers were content to adapt MerCAP to existing routines rather than use it to experiment with new directions, such as holding community forums to elicit the support and perspectives of parents and community-based organizations.

As evaluators, our frustration with the inability of the data to inform program adjustments was mirrored in what we heard from some frontline staff:

> This still looks more like a sanction program than like a service program. That's something we're finding in a lot of the welfare reform programs. It was very frustrating. Because you could see a lot of problems in homes—dysfunctionality, social problems, other problems causing attendance problems—yet we did nothing to ameliorate those problems. I was fuming because we were doing nothing. It was like beating my head against the wall.

Eventually we came to realize the role MerCAP played in the organizational identity of the county department among its statewide peers. Merced had long been known more for its persistently low social indicators than for innovative programs, but in this case it was the first county in California to implement a welfare school attendance program. As a result, MerCAP provided Merced officials a chance to be in the spotlight, including making presentations at statewide conferences attended by their peers. If only that understandable motivation and sense of pride had been better balanced with the reality check the metrics were offering, the program might have developed into something of which the locals might have been truly proud.

Writing for public planning professionals, John Forester (1999) argues for careful and imaginative listening to the stories told as publics gather. Forester insists that deliberative practice is not just about who gets to speak but who listens; how mutually, actively, and imaginatively; and with what degree of sensitivity to the underlying emotions, values, and meanings surfaced by the public encounter.

Rethinking Grant Reporting Requirements

When a funder provides a grant, a reporting relationship is created with the recipient. Formal written reports from grantees to funders—whether annual, quarterly, or otherwise—are a key ritual of modern governance. They take shape in the place where the two parties connect amid persistent conflicts generated by culture, rules, and scale. At issue is the nature of the connection being made, what it reveals or conceals, and what type of assessment or learning it makes possible.

Distance and distrust often produce a model concerned with rooting out embarrassing errors or celebrating apparent successes uncritically. Learning goals compete with others that often have a more immediate pull on funders, such as controlling corruption or claiming credit. It is a truism of the field of evaluation that the goals of retrospective assessment and continuous learning do not easily coexist, prompting debates among those emphasizing carefully constructed summative judgments (Scriven 1993) and those emphasizing a more developmental approach (Patton 2011).

Michel Foucault (2000) argued that reporting is an occasion for surveillance, the gaze of the master on those they control (Marquez 2012). In his view, it is a relationship among unequal parties in which power is associated with the achievement of precise and preordained purposes. The aim is to control uncertainty and unpredictability so that situations and people can be managed in ways that routine statistics can capture. The funder has resources the grantee needs and asserts power by deciding the terms and objectives of the grant. While it is also true that the funder needs the grantee to accomplish their objectives, they often have other applicants just as willing to accept the funds, or competing priorities to which resources can be shifted.

Under these conditions, grantee reports tend to put the best face on their efforts so as to increase the prospect of receiving future grants, short-circuiting open sharing about both success and failure. Evaluations whose goal is finding success stories or best-practice recommendations can exacerbate this problem. Often missing are serious efforts to confront failures or limitations or to understand how context and leadership shape what works, making replication difficult (Campbell, Carlisle-Cummins, and Feenstra 2013). What is needed is a more intentional commitment to learn from complex experiences. If organizations could build relationships with funders where they are rewarded for partnering with researchers and where the goal of the research is honest reflection rather than a search for "the one best way," we might see more progress.

We might hope that power imbalances and the dynamics of concealment in grantmaking relationships can be remedied by hiring external evaluators, the role I played in most of the projects I have been describing. But we do well to remember that most evaluators are also grantees and have their own reporting relationships with the funders. Even evaluators of high integrity face the reality I encountered throughout my work: if funders do not like what you have to say (or sometimes even if they do), they can choose to ignore it.

It would be particularly helpful for funders, evaluators, and project leaders to discuss results accountability issues jointly at the inception of projects, carefully balancing concerns for utility, feasibility, and cost. In addition to discussing the "upward accountability" of grantees to funders, these conversations should also include the "downward accountability" of funders to grantees. At a minimum, discussion of this kind would help to create an atmosphere of less anxiety and a greater sense of flexibility and experimentation toward achieving the civic purposes for which the grants were made.

Evaluators can potentially serve as helpful mediators or facilitators of these types of conversations, but only if they are brought into the process early enough and if the funders and grantees build a relationship that supports such a conversation. If the consistent laments of evaluation professionals can be trusted, this is not often the case.

Casting Evaluators as Facilitators of Democratic Learning

Evaluators are trained to look not simply at whether the intended effects of an intervention come to fruition but at whether there are unintended consequences as well. In conducting evaluations, I needed peripheral vision, to look not only at what a particular evaluation design brought into view but at the broader community and human consequences as these played out over time. Foveal vision, where our eyes are immediately focused, is associated with a type of tunnel vision that promotes anxious worrying and frantic energy. It is at odds with the spirit of deliberative inquiry, tending to lack a sense of context and perspective. By contrast, the value of peripheral vision is in bringing to awareness what isn't immediately apparent and framing the objects of immediate focus in a bigger picture.

How can this evaluative peripheral vision manifest itself with greater regularity? One approach is to view grants to communities as an intervention by an outside entity in a local context. Such grants necessarily interrupt some aspects of the ongoing flow of local energy and activity, while introducing others. A grant may also make certain new civic opportunities come to light, just waiting to be seized. The question to ask is "Does the process advance the stated civic purpose beyond what previous efforts have achieved, revealing new openings, or will it distract, deflect, or undermine existing efforts?"

A second approach is to give interviewees the space to tell you what is going on in their own terms. When I first began conducting evaluations with Joan Wright, she provided a pointed rebuke after watching me conduct an interview with a local official. Her critique was that I was too eager to show the interviewee how much I knew, too willing to answer the interviewee's question to me, "I assume you have heard about X, Y, or Z," with "Of course." Joan argued for playing dumb: "You never will find out what they really mean or learn anything new if you don't let them tell you." Her advice hit home for me and became a key part of my approach to interviewing from that point forward. Beyond the minimum necessary to convince interviewees that you are an intelligent listener, the rule of thumb is to let them fill in the details. These details often flesh out parts of the story that standard program evaluation questions would have missed.

This interviewing strategy may seem innocuous enough, but in my experience it was tied to a much broader approach to how university-trained scholars relate to the public. At the heart of this approach is being a learner rather than a possessor of knowledge. Learning is a process rooted in relationship and dialogue. In this sense, it is inherently democratic. By contrast, the person who knows something is always at risk of imposing the fruits of that knowledge on others or of treating their knowledge as a ticket to a special status rather than as an obligation to share and inform. If held too tightly, this expert stance disrupts something critical to a functioning civil society, a certain presumption of basic equality no matter the reality of any observable differences in talent or material circumstance.

In his 2007 presidential address to the American Evaluation Association, Thomas Schwandt lamented "the substitution of spin for reasoned assessment" (Schwandt 2008, 140). At stake is whether evaluators and other educators are cultivating the basic reasoning skills that a democracy requires: the ability to use evidence to assess reality, to suspend judgment while this evidence emerges and while different perspectives on its meaning are heard, and to weigh how much is enough as we navigate the inevitable trade-offs between different valued ends. Schwandt parts ways with those who believe that we can form democratic policy judgments based solely on the approach of evidence-based practice, in which we only invest in those approaches that have met some rigid standard of scientific verifiability. But neither does he believe we are stuck with the view that anyone's judgment is as good as anyone else's. Instead, he argues that evaluation has to work both from the top down (funder intent) and the bottom up (participant-oriented evaluation).

As we do the difficult work of forming public judgment amid complex realities and in the face of limited evidence, we are in a world of "satisficing" and "bounded rationality" (Lindblom 1959, 1979). The enemy, says Schwandt (2008, 144), is managerialism, which replaces the experimenting society with the audit society: "Society comes to take for granted the framing of policies and programs within the dominant managerial discourse," rather than pursuing a just society through debate, questioning, and deliberation. From this perspective, what comes to light as we engage in results accountability is just the beginning of an argument about moral and political value, not the end point. Thinking and acting in this way is what intelligent citizenship looks like.[9]

My experience conducting evaluations points in the direction of a broader and more politically aware manner of thinking about the work of policy analysis and program evaluation. Those of us working in these traditions would do well to focus not only on our role in providing objective interpretation but also on our participation in a democratic process taking place across the center-periphery divide. As it turns out, we are not just witnesses to the troubled marriage of metrics and mētis; we help write its script. Our analysis and reports explicitly or implicitly mediate the symbolic and practical concerns that divide bureaucratic funders and local grantees.

To do this work carefully requires more than just technical skill; it calls on our ability to establish trusting relationships, to communicate in ways that are clear and honest, and to be comfortable with the idea that we share power with many others, including those whose values diverge from our own. In my own attempts to navigate and inform funder and grantee perspectives, I became something like a marriage counselor, mirroring back to the troubled couple the nature of the tensions they were experiencing but also pointing with hope toward steps they might take to build a more mutually satisfying relationship.

Results Accountability and the Courage to Face Reality

Over time, I came to view results accountability less as a teachable technique or tool and more as a *practice* or *form*—a demanding standard or aspirational ideal to which we owe a citizenly obligation (Berry 1983; Levine 2015; MacIntyre 2007). In closing this chapter, I want to say a few words about what this shift in emphasis implies. Following the example set by Carol Levine (2015), I will draw on literary and artistic conceptions of form to inform our understanding of power. In this case, our concern is with the type of practical power and everyday heroism that results accountability must elicit if it is to succeed as a tool of governance.

Drawing examples from poetry and marriage, Wendell Berry argues that a *form* "is a way of accepting and living within the limits of creaturely life. . . . There are, it seems, two Muses: the Muse of Inspiration, who gives us inarticulate visions and desires, and the Muse of Realization, who returns again and again to say, 'It is more difficult than you thought.' This is the muse of form" (1983, 96). A *form* acts as container in which the exercise of discretion confronts limits but also is free to experiment, play, and learn. Consider, for example, the *form* we call jazz, where adherence to standard conventions provides the structure that enables the free-flowing improvisation for which jazz is so famous.[10]

The conventions of poetry, marriage, or jazz simultaneously limit and free us if we pay them due respect. The end result is not necessarily an easy path to success. Instead, *form* connects us to a difficulty by which we attend to what is real and true, both in the world and in our relationships. As Berry puts it: "Forms join the diverse things that they contain; they join their contents to their context; they join us to themselves; they join us to each other" (1983, 105).

At its best, results accountability as *form* takes policy out of the realm of pure intention and places it artfully and responsibly in the world. In the places of difficult achievement where metrics meet mētis, policy implementation finds its true vocation and we find our common work as civic agents using practical reason. When respected as a demanding form, results accountability enhances our collective competence, wedding the necessity of central policy formation to the corresponding discipline of respecting the individuality of particular places and people. Rightly understood, it is the proper name of the governance practice by which error can be recognized and good work celebrated and extended. Better system outcomes become more likely, generated jointly by professionals located in central bureaucracies and civic leaders rooted in local communities, both of whom see themselves as citizens before they are anything else.

At its worst, results accountability is an empty ritual of grant reporting or a mindless instrument of managerial control. An account is rendered that nods to excellent intentions and the gods of success, but without reference to resistance and difficulty, to the demands of the work's context, to the history of the places and people it is attempting to change, or to the impact on the ongoing ability of civic communities to carry out collective projects. Rather than sparking creative adaptations, reporting often short-circuits it, either by deliberate attempt or by the lack of an institutional process ensuring that reflection from diverse perspectives takes place.

The story turns on whether results thinking is pursued simply as a bureaucratic imperative, driven by the desire for external goods, or is instead practiced with the internal commitments, outlooks, and skills of democratic citizens (MacIntyre 2007). Are "results" simply the compelled currency of the new governance realm, inevitably subject to gaming and manipulation? Or are we, in our individual roles as bureaucrats or community change agents, voluntarily and internally motivated to learn from experience irrespective of immediate external rewards?

This latter possibility may indeed bring rewards and satisfactions but begins elsewhere in the courage to face reality head-on. It requires that we be open to the possibility of tragic conflict between competing goals, the discouragement of missing or ambiguous data, and the not-infrequent reluctance of human beings to change course even when the lesson of experience is clear.

7

Marshaling Hidden Hero Leadership

At the complex interface where bureaucracy and community networks meet—and amid the difficulties created by culture, rules, and scale—the hidden heroes turn recurring structural dilemmas into practical, actionable approaches that move the policy process forward. They exercise a vital if often overlooked form of practical power. As summarized in Table 7.1, we have been particularly concerned with *how* they do this.

In probing hidden hero stories, we have noted both the concrete practices they deploy and also a distinctive frame of reference they bring to their work—an ability to hold tension and embrace contraries (Elbow 1986). The larger point of view and the specific practices work hand in hand to create possibilities where others perceive roadblocks. Successful policy implementation—reliant on both bureaucratic resources and responsive community networks—is built on these pillars of perspective and practical power.

By focusing on the everyday practices of people who must marry metrics and mētis, we have revealed a distinct way of thinking about how the policy results we desire are created. We have also learned why achieving those outcomes is more difficult than we might like.

TABLE 7.1. HOW HIDDEN HEROES REFRAME RECURRING DILEMMAS IN EVERYDAY PRACTICE

Source of tension	Recurring dilemmas	Practical, actionable reframing
Culture	Bureaucracy vs. Community	Become conversant in both mentalities
	Metrics vs. mētis as essential and essentially incompatible	Honor and balance alternative forms of knowledge
	Expertise vs. local knowledge	Emphasize crossover roles: experts as community members, community members as experts
	Formal vs. relational styles	Create relationship-building occasions across divides; emphasize shared interests and distinct assets
	Rigid vs. experimental approaches	Build funding agendas/strategies from top down *and* bottom up, emphasizing learning and adaptation
Rules	Central control vs. Local discretion	Craft workarounds
	Consistency/fairness vs. fit to people and place	Treat rules as starting points for negotiation
	Material incentives from external funders vs. civic purposes generated within communities	Establish local networks as an alternative locus of accountability
	Accountability for funds vs. creative service integration	Differentiate front-door services from backdoor accounting
	Outcomes focus vs. compliance with rules and regulations	Use performance to justify discretion
Scale	Program-centric vs. multiscalar lenses	Exercise scalar imagination
	Program outcomes vs. community-scale indicators	Create conversations linking program indicators to community-scale outcomes
	Role of community networks, client codetermination, and civic time in generating outcomes vs. programs alone	View programs in light of local network dynamics while accounting for client codetermination and taking a longer time frame into account
	Accumulating measures and reports vs. taking time to reason about their meaning	Move deliberative processes inside institutions and grantmaking processes, debating the meaning of data from multiple perspectives

The parties to a results accountability relationship confront the tension of aspiration: the desire to do something of broad public value. To be able to say, "We did it, and our doing it made a difference." To aspire is to confront the reality of our limits: of time, attention, funds, energy. Since we value more than one thing and not all values can be achieved at once, trade-offs are inevitable. Our aspirations lead directly to difficult choices for policy leaders.

What might scholars and practitioners learn from the choices the hidden heroes make as they navigate the tensions generated by culture, rules, and scale? How can the important leadership of the hidden heroes become less hidden, more public, and more impactful in shaping the broader directions of public policy? How might their practices and larger point of view inform our theories of policy implementation? How might their experiences help us better prepare students in fields such as public administration, policy analysis, nonprofit management, or community development?

Four broad lessons emerge from the stories of hidden hero leadership, including the need to do the following:

- Rethink policy implementation strategies
- Protect hidden hero roles and functions
- Supplement technical training with a dialectical way of seeing
- View hidden hero power as active citizenship

Rethink Policy Implementation Strategies

Public or private initiatives designed to help disadvantaged communities have typically relied on top-down, short-term interventions. However well intended, these interventions inevitably treat the community's health and well-being as something that can be enhanced by a series of disconnected and expendable programs. What is lost in the process is the sense of the community as a working polity, a deliberative citizen body that over time is responsible for its own health and well-being.

The stories we have encountered suggest ways we might rethink policy implementation strategies to better honor the hidden heroes' contributions to democratic governance. A good first step is to acknowledge the role community networks play in achieving intended results. This stands in contrast to the too-narrow preoccupation with funding and assessing individual programs in isolation from one another and with little regard for community context.

Support Community Networks and Planning

Our research findings are consistent with a growing body of research suggesting that sprinkling a few short-term grants into communities is not the optimal strategy for realizing broader social policy goals (DiIulio 2007; Wineburg 2001). For example, in evaluating welfare and workforce development programs, we learned that the multifaceted needs of the poor are seldom met by a single organization or program. Instead, results are the creations of well-functioning networks of community care, along with the agency of clients themselves as nurtured in codetermination relationships. It makes sense to have multiple points of entry into a service delivery system and well-coordinated arrangements for client referrals between agencies—what some local areas call a "no wrong door" system.

Workaround stories suggest that the hidden heroes facilitate intended outcomes, despite the need to overcome rules, regulations, and accountability requirements that—in their totality—become contradictory and burdensome. The pursuit of workarounds, waivers, or other local accommodations that fit policy to place can be done poorly or well, and policy analysis is the poorer if these community-based dynamics are excluded from view.

Currently, few government contracts or foundation grants target the community as a unit of analysis or identify the provision or fortification of community civic space as an important goal. Nor does government funding regularly support broad-based community planning. Yet the vitality and health of community networks are as determinative of social policy outcomes than the variables on which policy analysts typically focus. As a general rule, social policy will benefit from paying more attention to building strong network connections and relationships among many diverse organizations rather than seeking the holy grail of the "one best provider" or becoming focused on a single evidence-based practice. Moving in this direction will require rethinking many aspects of policy implementation.

For example, by focusing the results accountability gaze almost exclusively on program outcomes, we miss opportunities to use metrics in ways that might better inform medium-to-long-term efforts to improve public policy and programs. As we learn from the Tillamook case discussed in the previous chapter, comparative community-level data can be enormously useful in identifying communities that fall above or below the norm, sparking local action or comparative learning. Metrics can also, over time, reveal larger patterns of change. It helps, for example, to know that we are spending ten times less on workforce development programs today than we were in the late 1970s (Giloth 2004, 2–3). These are all time-tested uses of social statistics or financial metrics, but they are seldom found within the narrowly gauged world of outcomes assessment as it plays out in center-to-periphery grants.

Another example is how grantee capacity building is defined and practiced. Even the otherwise exemplary capacity-building efforts of the Employment Development Department's Special Projects Team failed to fully embrace the community as the unit of analysis. The type of organization and grant-specific capacity building they practiced—typical of most top-down state and federal initiatives—does little to promote locally effective network development, for at least three reasons. First, its primary aim is to ensure that grantees can meet grant reporting requirements effectively, not to promote community collaboration. Second, working with a small subset of organizations in any given community misses the more promising opportunity of working on a community-wide scale to raise mutual awareness and create organizational linkages among *all* relevant organizations. Finally, a top-down approach that awards grants on the basis of limited information carries a high risk of allocating public resources to organizations lacking long-term partnership potential.

Basing partnership choices at the local level will not remove all the uncertainty, but it brings into play useful local knowledge about organizations and their leaders while also creating options for forms of collaboration that do not require external grants. It is just this type of knowledge that the hidden heroes often possess. As a result, any move away from program-centric policy implementation to support community network development is likely to make the work of the hidden heroes more visible and pivotal.

Honor Civic Passion and Policy Commitments

The hidden hero stories suggest one additional consideration for how policy is crafted, implemented, and evaluated. For obvious reasons, the material incentives tied to performance measures play a key role in shaping local policy implementation. However, to focus solely on this driver is to miss a separate motivation of behavior, one driven more by local civic purposes than by bureaucratic fiscal incentives. Journalists and policy analysts have been trained to "follow the money," but it is also important to follow the passion.

For example, in the workforce development system the hidden heroes know that the declining base of federal formula funding is not sufficient, by itself, to attract the ongoing engagement of civic leaders. By contrast, broader coalitions animated by civic purposes can draw on workforce system resources while also attracting a range of other public and private foundation funding. In the process, these civic coalitions become perceived as "the place where things are happening" in a local community, as was the case in Henry's region of California.

To free local workforce boards and One-Stop leaders to see themselves as community catalysts rather than solely as implementers of preset federal programs, a healthier balance of metrics and mētis is needed. One helpful approach would be to complement federally imposed performance measures with measures tied to strategic policy choices made in specific locales. This would allow local systems integration to be more focused and effective while continuing to discipline activity by promoting continuous learning (Gardner 2005). The most successful local workforce areas we studied took full advantage of the discretionary language in legislation to apply creative, entrepreneurial decision-making to the unique history, assets, and relationships that mark their communities. Our research uncovered a variety of these locally derived priorities: pursuing educational reforms to improve the quality of the local workforce; finding pathways to living-wage jobs for residents of impoverished neighborhoods; helping local youth do public work while becoming productive citizens; and supporting local economic sectors that provide high-wage jobs.

To be sure, we need programs, and there is a role for well-done program evaluations. That said, the conclusion to which my body of work points is that, by placing organizations and their programs at the center and relegating concern for community networks to the periphery, government and foundation grants that seek to redress poverty or improve community health have missed an important opportunity to build local partnerships that work from a program-participant, organizational, and community perspective.

A critic might argue that this sensitivity to the importance of community-level analysis was not a finding of my research so much as a presumption that I took into it. Indeed, my approach did reflect both my academic training and the way my role was defined as a community development Cooperative Extension Specialist. But I did not simply invent what I saw with the analytic lens I brought; the data were there to be seized. In the California faith-based initiative, nonprofit executive directors who spent more time in community networking were more likely to see their organizations develop into trusted government partners. In MerCAP, a promising idea faltered when legalistic implementation approaches treated welfare families one at a time and with suspicion, forfeiting the opportunity to enlist community supports that might have made the program more than an empty showcase.

Protect Hidden Hero Roles and Functions

Both our political culture and our political economy place great pressure on the very people we need to navigate the metrics-mētis divide. While devolution and results-based accountability nominally embrace local discretion, neoliberal policies and associated government spending reductions have weakened its practice. Downsizing often eliminates layers of middle managers who can use their experience and roots to "tap deep into the community's culture and sometimes put aside standard and prescribed ways of doing things" (Morgan et al. 1996, 362; Sennett 2006). These managers make essential, context-specific judgments about when and how to grant exceptions to the rules: adjudicating conflicts between community standards and those of the state or profession, interpretively navigating the jumble of potentially applicable rules or laws in a given case, and ensuring accountability to the overall socioeconomic well-being of the community.

Middle managers play the critical role in negotiating "the tension between those at the bottom of the organization, who are inclined to use particular standards to define good service (i.e., the ability to meet the needs of each individual served), and those at the top, who are inclined to use more formulaic metrics (i.e., average clients serviced, the greatest cost/benefit ratio, the total number of tasks performed/clients served, etc.)" (Morgan et al. 1996, 361–362). Over time, these managers accrue tacit knowledge akin to that of a doctor in clinical practice or a judge interpreting the law's applicability to a particular case. Local knowledge is particularly critical for social service networks facing nonroutine tasks, such as improving community health outcomes or finding jobs for the hard-to-employ. In these cases, client and community sensitivity, relationship building, codetermination, and linkage development become critical to making policy work as intended (Benjamin 2012; Benjamin and Campbell 2015; Campbell 2012).

If the governance dilemmas this book has explored were to be more widely recognized, we might expect to see more job descriptions like Maricela's, whose story we shared in the opening chapter. As it stands, there are comparatively few public or nonprofit jobs whose focus is systems alignment or navigation. Instead, results accountability requirements and compliance demands are being managed by people like the youth providers in Maricela's community or her bosses who routinely interface with federal officials but lose contact with grassroots organizations. Having someone like Maricela to navigate between the two worlds is a luxury that few organizations can boast but many need.

We also might hope to see more effective partnerships linking community organizers with bureaucratic insiders. As we learned in Chapter 3, public managers appreciate community organizers' ability to put political pressure on elected officials, ensuring that social and workforce development services are well funded in budget processes. These organizers can also educate decision-makers about community realities from which they are distanced. In these types of insider-outsider partnerships, the human work of juggling metrics and mētis is taking place, blending community intentions with the realities of rules, roles, and distant accountabilities.

The goal of elevating community voice can only be achieved by walking through the challenging terrain of complex organizations and their extended chains of command, reaching far beyond particular localities. Too often, we direct distrust and disapproval at the very people who are needed to build bridges and relationships within and beyond the local community. Staff work by bureaucrats is essential in a world in which community governance is heavily shaped by nonlocal influences, particularly external funding. Local public managers are one key link to these broader influences. So are local nonprofit leaders who avail themselves of broader networks in their region, state, or beyond. So are foundation staff who take an ongoing interest in a particular community but have ties to nonlocal sources of funding and to larger debates in society. Rather than castigating these institutional players as part of the problem, it makes sense to treat them as key community resources, finding ways to support and inform their work.

While they are busy being the hidden heroes of democratic agency, the public often refers to middle managers and frontline staff by another name: bureaucrat. As Bernardo Zacka (2017, 1) notes, "It is not a compliment . . . the word evokes rigidity, narrow-mindedness, insensitivity, coldness, lack of initiative, and, above all, rule-worship." As we have seen, such caricatures are not adequate in describing the human beings involved or the realities they face. Eliasoph (2011, 242) provides a succinct, colorful counterpoint: "Stodgy bureaucrats who worked side-by-side in their dusty offices for years usually developed habitual methods of getting things done." By positing these sometimes-stodgy bureaucrats and community leaders as partners in achieving civic purposes, jointly facing ingrained obstacles and the situation at hand, we begin to frame a more adequate and empowering picture of how policy can succeed.

Supplement Technical Training with a Dialectical Way of Seeing

The hidden heroes need technical skills, but more fundamentally they must develop a dialectical way of seeing. The technical skills—such as cost-benefit analysis, zero-based budgeting, asset-based community development, and network mapping—offer practical levers to act on the world. But the tools cannot be used without a deep appreciation of their limits and the complexities surrounding their use. By treating governance work as a craft practice, requiring a certain frame of mind in addition to technical competence, we find a better starting point for the training of public administrators, nonprofit managers, community developers, or grassroots organizers.

The dialectical point of view is anchored by the belief that "contraries can interact productively instead of fruitlessly fighting or conflicting with each other" (Elbow 1986, 233). One does not have to embrace Hegelian determinism—asserting that the tension of opposites will always lead to a better synthesis—to follow this path. Indeed, the hidden hero experiences do not support such simple optimism. Instead, they offer a hopeful realist perspective. Contraries *can* interact productively, but only if we act creatively within governance spaces marked by tension and conflict. As Gareth Morgan (1986, 258) notes: "Social arrangements generate inner contradictions that defeat the purposes for which they were set up," but we are not resigned to merely accepting this fate. Instead, leaders can "reframe the tensions and oppositions underlying the forces shaping the system, and thereby influence their direction" (266).

The way we organize our fields of study can unwittingly exacerbate the tendency to adopt simplified or polarized views in which contradictions may be bemoaned but not faced squarely. For example, my two primary academic homes, public administration and community development, both see themselves as promoting democratic agency—the ability of people to work together, across differences in values and perspectives, to solve public problems and realize public intentions. But their underlying assumptions about how to do so directly conflict. Public administration typically places its faith in trained professionals or experts, deemed necessary because the scale and complexity of problems in modern societies are beyond the capacity of ordinary citizens to understand or manage. A contrasting belief of community developers is the need to honor the voice and wisdom of local people since one-size-fits-all solutions imposed from above will flounder when applied bluntly to particular places and people. These abstractly cast distinctions are each true enough. But they are better at differentiating each field than in helping them to talk constructively at their common boundary.[1]

Students in these fields would benefit from exposure to key assumptions from the other discipline, a type of theoretical cross-training that academic programs might encourage. There are a variety of ways this could be done, including reading classic works from the other field, hearing directly from experienced hidden heroes, or being exposed to work around stories. Emphasizing training in navigational skills—broadly considered—is another approach. I mean by this the skills in cultural translation, rule negotiation, network development, and scalar imagination that play such a large role in defining the leadership of the hidden heroes. Direct exposure to these skills and governance dynamics via internship experiences is another approach, particularly if accompanied by reflection that requires students to recognize and address structural contradictions and the inevitability of trade-offs.

In teaching we often use concepts like "state" or "community" as if they were static, unified, and mutually exclusive. Students trying to find their way amid organizational complexity will not be well served by such a tidy demarcation of the policy world. Standing with a foot in both worlds, the hidden heroes demonstrate the degree to which state and community interpenetrate as policy is implemented. The idea is not completely new, of course. Much of the research on governance in the past few decades has documented the blurring of sectoral boundaries (Gronbjerg and Smith 2021; Wolch 1990). But even this literature seldom emphasizes the degree to which middle managers—public and nonprofit—find themselves simultaneously in both vertically organized hierarchies and horizontally organized community networks. As we have seen, it is this tension that defines the governance space in which the hidden heroes find themselves.

Not all their colleagues embrace the tension. For some, operating by the book keeps them in their superior's good graces but causes local collaborators to view them as bad partners. For others, loyalty to the local network or collaborative becomes the priority. These officials tend to be viewed suspiciously by their superiors in the vertical chain of command. The presence of these competing stances helps explain a phenomenon we observed regularly throughout our fieldwork. Different local areas had widely divergent experiences with the same state agency, primarily on the basis of how flexible the local agents of that agency were willing to be in implementing top-down directives. Students and policy scholars will benefit from paying closer attention to the variety of these stances and their influence on implementation dynamics.

View Hidden Hero Power as Active Citizenship

The grantmaking processes that this book has examined are animated by a shared purpose linking central funders and local implementers. As we have seen, however, what is shared sits among a host of other purposes and proclivities that are not shared at all. The practical power displayed by the hidden heroes is directed toward rescuing the shared purpose from the reality of difference. Which is to say, their work is a very human and challenging enterprise, for humans are purposeful creatures whose intentions routinely differ and align only with difficulty. This is the hard work of democracy.

I want to close by making the case that the hidden heroes exemplify more than simply enlightened management or exemplary administrative practice. In navigating a landscape of misaligned purposefulness, the hidden heroes demonstrate the promise and limits of active citizenship. A good starting point is the work of Jacques Ellul, the most determined critic of modern society's tendency to deny the freedom of our birthright, the creative agency that makes us human and undergirds democracy as a way of life. He denounces the idol of *technique*, which subsumes all of social reality to the logic of instrumental reason in a relentless search for the one mathematically best way to do things. Not only does this wrest agency and autonomy from its proper location in human beings but it warps what we mean when we appeal to "results":

> Whatever is effective, whatever possesses in itself an "efficiency," is justified. By applying means, a result is produced. This result is judged by the simplistic standard of "more": larger, faster, more precise, and so on. Simply by applying this criterion, the means is declared good. What succeeds is good, what fails is bad. (Ellul 2016, 45)

Technique in Ellul's sense writes intentionality, mētis, and moral judgment out of the governance process altogether. The value of particularity is eclipsed by that of categorization so that the proper means can be applied to produce a given result.

As Charles Taylor (2007, 739, 740) puts it: "Rules prescribe treatments for categories of people, so a tremendously important feature of our lives is that we fit into categories; our rights, entitlements, burdens, etc. depend on these. These shape our lives, make us see ourselves in new ways, in which category-belonging bulks large, and the idiosyncratically-enfleshed individual becomes less relevant." The answer, says Taylor, is not to eliminate rules or codes, which we cannot escape or do without. But we must keep in mind their power to restrict our agency, understanding how their simplifications can foster actions taken without due concern for human consequences.

Elsewhere, Taylor (1991, 110–111) expresses the difficulty of modern governance in broader terms:

> Our challenge is actually to combine in some non-self-stultifying fashion a number of ways of operating, which are jointly necessary to a free and prosperous society but which also tend to impede each other: market allocations, state planning, collective provision for need, the defense of individual rights, and effective democratic initiative and control. . . . But this poses a problem, because the joint operation of market and bureaucratic state has a tendency to weaken democratic initiative.

The alternative, as argued by Alan Wolfe (1989, 212) and exemplified by the hidden heroes, is to remind ourselves that humans are active "rule makers" rather than simply "rule followers." We need to balance metrics with mētis because we want to "take context into account," we want to "assert the moral validity of particular claims," and we want to "allow for ambiguity in resolving unexpected dilemmas" (229). Neither market nor state rules—both characteristically static and universal—can deal with complexity and ambiguity in this iterative, purposeful fashion. Here we find a starting point for democratic accountability that has the potential to bring together a legitimate but not exclusive emphasis on results with our moral responsibility to self and others, rooted in the places where we live and the communities to whom we owe obligations and allegiance.

A shadow hangs over this vision of human agency, whatever our democratic hopes for it. The capacity to create carries with it the possibility of blundering. As Christopher Lasch (1984, 258–259) reminds us, being active as humans requires a moral capacity for remorse and regret, a desire to make amends or set things right. Properly under-

stood, results accountability can provide a container for this reflection, but only if exercised with a truth-telling humility that accepts
that we are never going to be free of error. Large-scale systems pose a
problem for this way of thinking—their scope of operation can turn
small errors into large embarrassments, and they operate without the
trust in which democratic humility can be seen as a virtue.

Here the tradition of antitechnological and antibureaucratic
thought confronts the hard reality of the modern world of large organizations and the Madisonian political system. Madison shared the
view of human fallibility expressed by Lasch and others but was trying to design a political system on a continental rather than a communal scale. Since people were not angels, he built the system "to
keep citizens apart" (Kemmis 1990), hoping that procedural mechanisms like the separation of powers, checks and balances, and time-
limited legislative calendars would allow government to transcend
human fallibility. Madison's proceduralism, like the self-correcting
free markets in Adam Smith's capitalism, would engineer social har-
mony without it having to be purposively pursued by human beings.
Instead, argues Daniel Kemmis, by taking citizen agency out of the
picture, Madison's system breeds the political stalemate and public
disillusionment that has given rise to the contemporary emphasis on
results by governance reformers.

Against this backdrop, the way the hidden heroes actively pursue
purposive results calls us to a renewed sense of democratic agency, to
the "dynamic repair" (Sennett 2008) or "developmental innovation"
(Patton 2011) that characterizes the work of people who face difficult
or ambiguous problems. Within public administration, this view has
been most forcefully articulated in Charles Lindblom's (1959, 1979)
theory of "muddling through" or "disjointed incrementalism," rooted in assumptions about the inherent limits of centralized intelligence and power, however much we also depend on those.

Three decades later, I emerge convinced that the metrics-mētis
riddle of essential and essentially incompatible ideas is one we must
not evade but imaginatively embrace. Paying attention to the landscape of difficulty occasioned by new governance experiments might
teach us a valuable lesson in humility, a recognition that not all our
problems are amenable to straightforward or total solutions (Sennett
2012, xi). It might also engender a certain patience with one another

where our loyalties diverge across the divide between bureaucratic hierarchies and organized communities or when our will to overcome the divide encounters stubborn, ingrained resistance.

Not all our dialogue about how to proceed may end in shared agreements or a clear action agenda, but we might hope that it makes us more aware of our misunderstandings, more open to listening empathetically to those with whom we disagree. Needless to say, these needed qualities have been in short supply in our political culture generally, a reality that I too often found mirrored in the relationships of funders and grantees with whom I engaged. Perhaps what can be learned from the hidden heroes can inform our broader approach to overcoming cultural polarization and the geography of isolation that pervades modern life.

Democracy places a high bar before us, but it rests on practices and roles that are within our reach. Meeting this bar requires that we each be willing to take on the responsibilities and obligations of active citizenship. This role is available to all of us—experts and laypersons, insiders and outsiders, veterans and newcomers. The hidden hero stories suggest that the public work we need can begin wherever we are, with whatever perspectives we bring, with whatever difficulties we face, and with whatever resources are at our disposal. It is our willingness and ability to bring to bear the assets we have to address the situation at hand that allows democratic agency to flourish, rather than any particular ideological bent, special skill set, or currently vogue managerial or participatory technique. The demanding work of citizenship is doable because what we need is already here: here in the resources of our people and institutions if we can only animate them with meaning, character, and purpose.

If democracy today is about results, we need to remember the Greek understanding of power as the capacity to achieve purpose. The hidden heroes remind us that this form of power is always a matter of scale, proportion, and fit. It grows out of right relationship and embodied experience in the face of the contingent nature of all life, bonding us to our fellow citizens. Abstraction is the enemy of the good if it routinely substitutes contextless numbers for informed professional and community judgment. Particularity also can lead us astray, undermining the legitimate claims of central policy formation or the need to preserve and protect the space for community politics in a globally integrated world. No formula—of results accountability or any other—will, by itself, reconcile metrics and mētis. If there is to be a healthy marriage of the two, it will be because we do it, together, engaging one another with presence, humility, and care.

We do it, and our doing it makes the difference.

Appendix

This appendix provides a basic profile of the eight evaluation projects from which most of this book's case examples are drawn. Readers seeking more detailed information on particular projects are encouraged to consult the listed articles and evaluation reports.

Government-Funded Projects

California Community and Faith-Based Initiative (CFBI)

Policy Focus
Workforce development

Goals
- To expand access to workforce development services among hard-to-employ populations
- To develop the capacity of grantees to function as government partners

Funding Amount/Duration/Source
$17 million (to 40 nonprofits)/3years/CA Employment Development Department (EDD)

Implementing Agencies
Local community and faith-related organizations; EDD Special Projects team

Setting/Scope within California
Funded organizations could be found in diverse settings in most regions across the state

Evaluation Goals/Purposes
- To learn how programs identify, recruit, train, and support employment
- To understand the roles community- and faith-related organizations play in local workforce development networks
- To explore how staff and participants in funded programs define success

Key Methods/Activities
Outcome analysis of all 40 grantees and comparative case studies of 14 nonprofits:

- 277 interviews (134 with participants)
- 46 organizational surveys
- 24 site visits

Evaluation Funding/Duration/Source
$304,000/3 years (2002–2005)/California EDD

Journal Articles and Link to Evaluation Report
Benjamin and Campbell 2015; Campbell and Glunt 2006; Campbell 2011b, 2016
http://ucanr.edu/sites/UC_CCP/files/125972.pdf

Implementation of the Workforce Investment Act in California

Policy Focus
Workforce development and community economic development

Goals
- To create and maintain employment resource centers (One-Stops)
- To provide formal training services to those eligible
- To provide business services
- To work with partners to coordinate the One-Stop system
- To meet standards on 17 federally mandated performance measures

Funding Amount/Duration/Source
Various federal agencies allocate $4–5 billion annually (California Budget Project 2005)

Implementing Agencies
Local Workforce Investment Boards and their community partners
California Labor and Workforce Development Agency
California Employment Development Department

Setting/Scope within California
Statewide program with funds allocated to 50 Local Workforce Investment Boards

Evaluation Questions
- What is the operative mission of the workforce development system?
- How adequate are system resources, and how are dollars allocated for various purposes?
- What services/programs are offered and what types of job seekers/businesses are served?
- What patterns characterize the relationships of key partners in the system?
- What mechanisms exist to promote coordinated planning and service integration?

Key Methods/Activities
Comparative case studies of 10 local workforce areas (Alameda County, Los Angeles City, the Northern Rural Training and Employment Consortium [NoRTEC], the city of Oakland, Sacramento County, San Bernardino County, Southeast Los Angeles County [SELACO], Sonoma County, Tulare County, and Verdugo):

- 297 interviews
- 69 back-end surveys
- 30 site visits
- around 60 meeting observations

Evaluation Funding/Duration/Source
$375,000/3 years (2004–2006)/California Labor and Workforce Development Agency

Journal Articles and Links to Evaluation Reports
David Campbell 2011a, 2012; https://ucanr.edu/sites/UC_CCP/files/125931.pdf; https://ucanr.edu/sites/UC_CCP/files/125927.pdf

Implementation of Workforce Investment Act (WIA) Youth Programs in California

Policy Focus
Youth workforce development

Goals
- To help youth make effective transitions to higher education and careers
- To select and oversee youth service providers/contracts
- To support coordination among local youth-serving organizations

Funding Amount/Duration/Source
The 10 local workforce areas we studied received approximately $33 million in WIA formula funding annually for youth services in 2003–2004.

Implementing Agencies
Local Workforce Investment Boards, youth councils, and their community partners; California Labor and Workforce Development Agency; California Employment Development Department

Setting/Scope within California
Statewide program with funds allocated to 50 Local Workforce Investment Boards

Evaluation Goals/Purposes
- To investigate how WIA youth provisions are being implemented in local areas
- To generate evidence about what is working and what is not
- To provide insight that might inform policy and program planning

Key Methods/Activities
Comparative case studies of 10 local-area youth councils and youth programs (Los Angeles City, Merced County, NoRTEC, Orange County, San Joaquin County, city of Santa Ana, Solano County, Sonoma County, Tulare County, and Verdugo):
- 104 interviews (6 with youth on youth councils)
- 8 focus groups with 59 youth participants
- around 20 meeting observations

Evaluation Funding/Duration/Sources
$64,000/2 years (2005–2006)/University of California ($34,000), and California Labor and Workforce Development Agency ($30,000)

Link to Evaluation Report
https://ucanr.edu/sites/UC_CCP/files/125928.pdf

Merced County Attendance Project (MerCAP)

Policy Focus
Welfare school attendance

Goals
- To reinforce norms of personal responsibility for parents and students
- To support school attendance
- To decrease future welfare dependency

Funding Amount/Duration/Source
None (except for evaluation)/3-year pilot/California Department of Social Services

Implementing Agencies
County human services agency; county schools

Setting/Scope within California
Merced County, a rural county in California's Central Valley with high levels of poverty

Evaluation Goals/Purposes
- To determine whether MerCAP improves school attendance and performance of Temporary Assistance for Needy Families (TANF) youth
- To determine whether MerCAP has an impact on parent interaction with schools
- To develop a qualitative understanding of the kinds of family problems underlying absenteeism
- To obtain information on the costs of operating a school attendance program

Key Methods/Activities
Compared results across 71 participating public schools:

- Analysis of attendance and attendance actions data
- 490 interviews (372 with parents, mostly in focus groups)
- 20 meeting observations
- 71 school site visits/surveys

Evaluation Funding/Duration/Source
$295,000/3 years (1997–2000)/California Department of Social Services

Journal Article and Link to Evaluation Report
Campbell and Wright 2005; https://ucanr.edu/sites/UC_CCP/files/125943.pdf

Foundation-Funded Projects

Civic Engagement Project for Children and Families

Policy Focus
Promotion of civic engagement on behalf of young children (from birth to age five) and their families

Goals
- To obtain the broad public input in the creation of policy and programs for children from birth to age five

- To stimulate civic dialogue about early childhood development
- To learn lessons about meaningful civic engagement

Funding Amount/Duration/Source
$2 million/3 years/5 foundations: David and Lucile Packard, James Irvine, Miriam and Peter Haas Fund, Peninsula Community, and Walter and Elise Haas Fund

Implementing Agencies
Local Prop 10 (First Five) commissions and Civic Engagement Project staff

Setting/Scope within California
8 counties varying by urban/rural location, economic health, demographic make-up, and political orientation: Contra Costa, Monterey, San Diego, San Francisco, San Mateo, Santa Clara, Santa Cruz, and Yolo

Evaluation Questions
- What forms/tools of civic engagement did local commissions use?
- What ideas, expectations, and assumptions underlie these forms/tools?
- What outcomes and conditions support or limit the applicability of these forms/tools?

Key Methods/Activities
8 comparative case studies of local Prop 10 commissions:

- 340 interviews (132 with community participants)
- 148 meeting observations
- Document review
- Analysis of census data

Evaluation Funding/Duration/Sources
$180,000/3 years (1999–2002)/5 foundations: David and Lucile Packard, James Irvine, Peninsula Community, Miriam and Peter Haas, Walter and Elise Haas

Journal Article and Link to Evaluation Report
David Campbell 2010; https://ucanr.edu/sites/UC_CCP/files/364744.pdf

Community Planning and Advisory Council (ComPAC)

Policy Focus
Healthy communities

Goals
- Create a 501(c)(3) organization
- Establish measurable indicators of health, environment, education, and economy
- Initiate community projects

Funding Amount/Duration/Source
$225,000/3 years/California Endowment

Implementing Agency
Nonprofit newly formed by grant (ComPAC)

Setting/Scope within California
Small, isolated rural county undergoing demographic change

Evaluation Goals/Purposes
To engage participants in continuous learning in order to focus goals, reflect on the actions taken, assess progress, and chart direction

Key Methods/Activities
- 89 interviews
- 5 meeting observations
- Document review

Evaluation Funding/Duration/Source
$43,000/3 years (1997–1999)/Northeastern Rural Health Clinics (Note: evaluation funded jointly with Fitness Project evaluation)

Link to Evaluation Report
https://ucanr.edu/sites/UC_CCP/files/364745.pdf

Lassen Fitness Project

Policy Focus
Personal fitness and health education

Goals
- To increase community knowledge of the benefits of regular physical activity
- To increase regular physical activity
- To enlist businesses as partners

Funding Amount/Duration/Source
$220,000/3 years/James Irvine Foundation

Implementing Agency
The Lassen Wellness Center, part of a private, nonprofit health-care provider

Setting/Scope within California
Small, isolated rural county undergoing demographic change

Evaluation Goals/Purposes
To engage participants in continuous learning in order to focus goals, reflect on the actions taken, assess progress, and chart direction

Key Methods/Activities
- 89 interviews
- 5 meeting observations
- Document review

Evaluation Funding/Duration/Source
$43,000/3 years (1997–1999)/Northeastern Rural Health Clinics (Note: evaluation funded jointly with ComPAC evaluation)

Link to Evaluation Report
https://ucanr.edu/sites/UC_CCP/files/364746.pdf

REACH Youth Development

Policy Focus
Community youth development

Goals
- To build local youth-adult coalitions
- To provide meaningful engagement and leadership opportunities for youth
- To catalyze community and policy change benefiting youth

Funding Amount/Duration/Source
$8 million/5 years/Sierra Health Foundation

Implementing Agencies
Local youth development coalitions developed by nonprofits or schools

Setting/Scope within California
7 demographically diverse cities/neighborhoods in the Sacramento region: El Dorado Hills, Galt, Meadowview, Rancho Cordova, South Sacramento, West Sacramento, Woodland

Evaluation Questions
- Does REACH nurture viable coalitions and enhance community capacity to support youth?
- Does REACH engage youth in ways that enhance young people's skills, leadership, and community involvement?

- Does REACH catalyze meaningful community change strategies related to youth development?
- Does REACH increase meaningful supports and opportunities for youth in local communities?
- Does REACH suggest lessons for foundation practice and community youth studies?

Key Methods/Activities

Comparative case studies of 7 youth-adult coalitions in cities/neighborhoods:

- 346 interviews (87 with youth)
- 323 meeting observations
- Document and literature review

Evaluation Funding/Duration/Source

$375,000/3 years (2007–2010)/Sierra Health Foundation

Journal Article and Link to Evaluation Report

Campbell and Erbstein 2012; https://ucanr.edu/sites/UC_CCP/files/125983.pdf

Notes

Chapter 1

1. We promised anonymity to all our interviewees, so I have altered their names and other identifying details throughout the book.

2. Fiscal belt-tightening has hit workforce development programs particularly hard, despite this being a rare policy arena in which bipartisan agreement can be found. Taking inflation into account, the United States was spending almost ten times less for workforce programs in 2000 than it did in 1978 (Giloth 2004, 2–3).

3. I am using the word "hero" in the classic sense of a protagonist in a myth, tragedy, or epic. Heroes face challenges, often in a context that is unfair or where the odds are stacked against them. They act according to their own sense of what is right, drawing on skills and experience that others lack. They may succeed or fail in immediate terms, but they persist in the quest set before them.

4. In emphasizing results, my approach differs from scholarship that treats democratic agency primarily in terms of electoral participation or the mobilization of social movements (Dahl 1967). As recent events remind us, the importance of protest, the franchise, and the integrity of elections is indeed critical and should not be taken for granted. Nevertheless, there are important forms of democratic agency that do not fit easily into the categories of liberal democrats (focused on system-maintaining elections) or their critics (focused on system-challenging protests). These forms develop within the space in our governance processes where top-down and bottom-up forces awkwardly meet.

5. In an analogous fashion, ecologists have coined the term "ecotone" to describe a place where two natural ecologies meet. The word's Greek roots describe a "place of tension." Marshes are an example, as are the places where forests and grasslands rub up against one another. Scientists find that paying attention to ecotones clarifies the nature of the surrounding ecosystems and provides an early warning of impending environmental dangers (Risser 1995).

6. The Appendix provides an overview of these eight projects, links to related evaluation reports and journal articles, and information on our research goals, scope, and funding.

Chapter 2

1. In Greek mythology, Mētis is a Titan goddess. She is known as the mother of wisdom, prudence, and deep thought. To perfect his own power, Zeus marries Mētis, hoping to benefit from her cunning intelligence. But he soon grows fearful. The oracle has told him that their children—possessing both brute strength and sly wisdom—will have a power that eclipses his own. To remove the threat, Zeus turns Mētis into a fly and swallows her. It turns out that she is already pregnant with their daughter, Athena. In the belly of Zeus, Mētis prepares a helmet and robe for the daughter, and her hammer blows give Zeus a bad headache. To relieve his pain, Zeus has the god of forge and fire split open his forehead with an axe, releasing Athena. She becomes a teacher, instructing others in the everyday crafts of weaving, sewing, farming, and metalwork. The attempt to banish Mētis backfires on Zeus, and it is their joint offspring, Athena, who becomes the patron and protectress of the Greek capital: Athens, birthplace of democracy.

2. Writing to advise public and private mangers, Donald Schon (1983) provides the most forceful articulation of the view that good policy and practice requires more than adherence to expert-derived "best practices." As Joseph Dunne (1993, xiii) summarizes, Schon "draws attention to a considerable mismatch between an entrenched picture of the kind of science-based knowledge which successful practitioners are *supposed* to possess and the knowing-in-action which their practices actually embody." Whether termed "mētis" (Scott 1998), "phronesis" (Dunne 1993; Schwartz and Sharpe 2010), "thinking in time" (Neustadt and May 1986), "reading the situation" (Patton 2002), or "deliberative practice" (Forester 1999), this type of context-sensitive judgment is necessary to introduce democracy into the complex, nonroutine settings where bureaucracy and community meet.

3. I am grateful to Peter Levine for this insight.

Chapter 3

1. The study was conducted by postdoctoral scholar Kelsey Meagher working with Professor Edward Spang of the University of California, Davis, a project on which I served as a collaborator (Meagher, Campbell, and Spang 2022).

Between January and April 2021, Meagher interviewed thirty individuals from twenty-four hunger-relief organizations in California. Most of the respondents worked at food banks (n = 24), and the remaining individuals worked in food pantries, food distribution organizations, or government agencies. The hunger-relief organizations in the sample collectively serve twenty-eight of the fifty-eight counties in California, represent both urban and rural regions, and have operational capacities that range from serving less than 1,000 people per month with just a handful of paid staff to over 300,000 thousand per month with over one hundred paid staff.

Chapter 5

1. I am particularly grateful to my colleague Cathy Lemp for gaining the trust of the women and penning these vivid descriptions.

2. This section draws on research conducted jointly with my colleague Lehn Benjamin (Benjamin and Campbell 2015), who deserves credit for having framed our analysis and for providing many of the specific examples drawing on her independently conducted research.

3. This example draws from the evaluation Joan Wright and I conducted and on the subsequent work of Harder and Company, who finished the evaluation after Joan's retirement ended our involvement two years into the three-year project. For more, see Harder and Company (2004, 15–18) and Campbell (2010).

Chapter 6

1. Though separately funded and led, the fitness project was considered to be part of the umbrella of community projects associated with ComPAC. Our work as evaluators was jointly funded by the projects but resulted in two separate reports.

2. The foundation provided $220,000 for the project, spread over three years. Part of that funding was devoted to our evaluation, as in this case we were hired by the local project leaders rather than by the foundation.

3. After 1994, the county's teen pregnancy rates gradually rose to about the state average. In some versions of the story, this was due to a key leader moving away. Whether that is the case or not, shifting focus and attention is a typical feature of politics, one of the reasons reform is so difficult to maintain and sustain.

4. As noted by a colleague, the use of CitiStat by police "did nothing to surface, reflect on, and correct police violence in black communities. Only with Black Lives Matter activism did routine, racialized brutality become an unavoidable part of a long overdue public discussion of policing in this country." The point is well taken, serving as a reminder of the limits of any particular tool or a too-simple optimism about what the hidden heroes can and cannot do on their own.

5. I am grateful to Michael Patton for this formulation, which he offered on a panel at the American Evaluation Association in Denver, October 2014.

6. The section draws on Benjamin and Campbell 2015.

7. For more, see Charles Taylor's (2007, 737–743) illuminating discussion of Illich's interpretation of the Good Samaritan story.

8. Head lice was a particular problem in the county, prompting the county health agency to develop a "lice patrol" program featuring a mobile van and volunteer "nitpickers."

9. Richard Sennett (2008, 249) connects this approach to the idea of craftsmanship. He identifies three skills or moments in the craft ideal. First is the ability to *locate*: focusing attention on the particular situation, places where an important problem exists and matters. Second is the ability to *question*: engaging our curiosity as we explore what is going on here. Finally, there is the skill of suspending judgment in order to *open up*: probing alternative points of view and engaging in reasoning that moves back and forth from the particular to the abstract. This work need not be restricted to academics, with their relative freedom to explore ideas and see where they lead. Sennett believes the skills in question are broadly distributed because they draw on the basic capabilities of human beings, including the capacity for play.

10. In Frank Conroy's 1993 novel *Body and Soul*, he includes a remarkable passage in which two performers were "playing without any preconceived plan, relying on traditional jazz conventions." The conventions provide the form, disciplining their play: "breaking into 'fours,' for instance, at what felt like the appropriate moment. Four bars drum solo, four bars tutti, four bars bass solo, four bars tutti, and so on for two choruses." The players then begin "improvising contrapuntal lines . . . they spontaneously and simultaneously made a dramatic change in the harmonic structure." We learn that they "would later wonder how they could possibly have done something so radical, entirely by feel, at the same moment" (436).

Chapter 7

1. I would also acknowledge the many voices within each of these fields that are working to build the necessary bridges. My point here is simply to emphasize the often-unquestioned assumptions that make this bridge building difficult.

References

Ackerman, Bruce, and James S. Fishkin. 2004. *Deliberation Day*. New Haven, CT: Yale University Press.

Alinsky, Saul D. 1961. *Rules for Radicals: A Pragmatic Primer for Realistic Radicals*. New York: Vintage Books.

Allen, Patricia, and Julie Guthman. 2006. "From 'Old School' to 'Farm-to-School': Neoliberalization from the Ground Up." *Agriculture and Human Values* 23: 401–415.

Ambrose, Stephen E. 1997. *Citizen Soldiers*. New York: Simon and Schuster.

Ansell, Christopher K. 2011. *Pragmatist Democracy: Evolutionary Learning as Public Philosophy*. New York: Oxford University Press.

Ansell, Christopher K., and Alison Gash. 2008. "Collaborative Governance in Theory and Practice." *Journal of Public Administration Theory and Practice* 18 (4): 543–571.

Arnstein, Sherry R. 1969. "A Ladder of Citizen Participation." *Journal of the American Institute of Planners* 35 (4): 216–224.

Azad, Bijan, and Nelson King. 2008. "Enacting Computer Workaround Practices within a Medication Dispensing System." *European Journal of Information System* 15: 264–278.

Baiocchi, Gianpaolo. 2001. "Participation, Activism, and Politics: The Porto Alegre Experiment and Deliberative Democratic Theory." *Politics and Society* 29 (1): 43–72.

Ban, Carolyn. 1995. *How Do Public Managers Manage? Bureaucratic Constraints, Organizational Culture, and the Potential for Reform.* San Francisco: Jossey-Bass.

Bardach, Eugene. 1977. *The Implementation Game: What Happens After a Bill Becomes Law.* Boston: MIT Press.

———. 1998. *Getting Agencies to Work Together: The Practice and Theory of Managerial Craftsmanship.* Washington, DC: Brookings Institution.

Bass, G., and P. Lemmon. 1998. "Measuring the Measurers: A Nonprofit Assessment of the Government Performance and Results Act (GPRA)." Washington, DC: Nonprofit Sector Research Fund.

Behn, Robert D. 2001. *Rethinking Democratic Accountability.* Washington, DC: Brookings Institution.

———. 2010. "Reciprocity, Corruption, and Performance." *Bob Behn's Leadership Report* 8, no. 7 (March).

———. 2014. *The PerformanceStat Potential: A Leadership Strategy for Producing Results.* Washington, DC: Brookings Institution.

Benjamin, Lehn M. 2012. "Nonprofit Organizations and Outcome Measurement: From Tracking Program Activities to Focusing on Frontline Work." *American Journal of Evaluation* 33: 431–447.

Benjamin, Lehn M., and David C. Campbell. 2015. "Nonprofit Performance: Accounting for the Agency of Clients." *Nonprofit and Voluntary Sector Quarterly* 44 (5): 988–1006.

Berger, Peter, and John Neuhaus. 1977. *To Empower People: The Role of Mediating Structures in Public Policy.* Washington, DC: American Enterprise Institute.

Berry, Wendell. 1977. *The Unsettling of America.* San Francisco: Sierra Club Books.

———. 1983. *Standing by Words.* Berkeley, CA: Counterpoint.

Bettelheim, Bruno. 1967. *The Empty Fortress: Infantile Autism and the Birth of the Self.* New York: Free Press.

Boddie, Stephanie C., and Ram A. Cnaan. 2006. *Faith-Based Social Services: Measures, Assessments, Effectiveness.* Binghamton, NY: Haworth.

Boyte, Harry C. 1989. *Commonwealth: A Return to Citizen Politics.* New York: Free Press.

———. 2004. *Everyday Politics: Reconnecting Citizens and Public Life.* Philadelphia: University of Pennsylvania Press.

———. 2021. "The School Wars and the Empowerment Gap." Paper presented at the December 3–4, 2021, conference Civic Studies: The University as Civic Catalyst, St. Paul, Minnesota.

Boyte, Harry C., and Nancy N. Kari. 1996. *Building America: The Democratic Promise of Public Work.* Philadelphia: Temple University Press.

Bradshaw, Ted K., James R. King, and Stephen Wahlstrom. 1999. "Catching On to Clusters." *Planning* 65 (6): 18–22.

Braverman, Harry. 1974. *Labor and Monopoly Capital: The Degradation of Work in the Twentieth Century.* New York: Monthly Review.

Briggs, Xavier S. 2008. *Democracy as Problem-Solving: Civic Capacity in Communities across the Globe.* Cambridge, MA: MIT Press.

Brodkin, Evelyn Z., and Gregory Marston. 2013. *Work and the Welfare State: Street-Level Organizations and Workfare Politics.* Washington, DC: Georgetown University Press.

Bryan, Todd. 2004. "Tragedy Averted: The Promise of Collaboration." *Society and Natural Resources* 17: 881–896.

Buttel, Fred H. 1992. "Environmentalism: Origins, Processes, and Implications for Rural Social Change." *Rural Sociology* 57 (1): 1–27.

California Association of Food Banks. 2021. "Farm to Family." Accessed May 1, 2021. https://www.cafoodbanks.org/what-we-do/farm-family/.

California Budget Project. 2005. "Understanding California's Workforce Development System: A Comprehensive Compendium of Workforce Development Programs in California." Sacramento: California Budget Project.

Campbell, David. 2002. "Outcomes Assessment and the Paradox of Nonprofit Accountability." *Nonprofit Management & Leadership* 12 (3): 243–259.

———. 2010. "Democratic Norms to Deliberative Forms: Managing Tools and Tradeoffs in Community-Based Civic Engagement." *Public Administration and Management* 15 (1): 305–341.

———. 2011a. "Policy Workaround Stories Are Valuable Evaluative Indicators: But Should They Be Told?" *American Journal of Evaluation* 32 (3): 408–441.

———. 2011b. "Reconsidering the Implementation Strategy in Faith-Based Policy Initiatives." *Nonprofit and Voluntary Sector Quarterly* 40 (1): 130–148.

———. 2012. "Public Managers in Integrated Services Collaboratives: What Works Is Workarounds." *Public Administration Review* 72 (5): 721–730.

———. 2016. "Small Faith-Related Organizations as Partners in Local Social Service Networks." *Religions* 7 (57). Available at https://doi.org/10.3390/rel7050057.

Campbell, David, Ildi Carlisle-Cummins, and Gail Feenstra. 2013. "Community Food Systems: Strengthening the Research-to-Practice Continuum." *Journal of Agriculture, Food Systems, and Community Development* 3 (3): 121–138.

Campbell, David, and Nancy Erbstein. 2012. "Engaging Youth in Community Change: Three Key Implementation Principles." *Community Development* 43 (1): 63–79.

Campbell, David, and Gail Feenstra. 2001. "A Local Partnership for Sustainable Food and Agriculture: The Case of PlacerGROWN." In *Creating Sustainable Community Programs: Examples of Collaborative Public Administration,* edited by Mark R. Daniels, 205–220. Westport, CT: Praeger.

———. 2005. "Community Food Systems and the Work of Public Scholarship." In *Engaging Campus and Community: The Practice of Public Scholarship in the State and Land-Grant University System,* edited by Scott J. Peters, Nicholas R. Jordan, Margaret Adamek, and Theodore R. Alter, 37–65. Dayton, OH: Kettering Foundation.

Campbell, David, and Eric Glunt. 2006. "Assessing the Effectiveness of Faith-Based Programs: A Local Network Perspective." *Social Thought: Journal of Religion and Spirituality in Social Work* 25 (3/4): 241–259.

Campbell, David, and Cathy Lemp. 2007. *The Promise and Limits of Community and Faith-Related Organizations as Government Workforce Development Partners.* Final Evaluation Report of the California Community and Faith-Based Initiative. Davis: California Communities Program, University of California, Davis.

Campbell, David, Cathy Lemp, and Jeanette Trieber. 2006. "WIA Implementation in California: Findings and Recommendations." Davis, CA: California Communities Program, University of California, Davis.

Campbell, David, and Joan Wright. 2005. "Rethinking Welfare School-Attendance Policies." *Social Service Review* 79 (1): 2–28.

Carter, Neil, and Patricia Greer. 1993. "Evaluating Agencies: Next Steps and Performance Indicators." *Public Administration* 71: 407–416.

Cartwright, Nancy, and Jeremy Hardie. 2012. *Evidence-Based Policy: A Practical Guide to Doing It Better.* New York: Oxford University Press.

Christensen, Karen S. 1999. *Cities and Complexity: Making Intergovernmental Decisions.* Thousand Oaks, CA: Sage.

Cobb, Clifford W., and Craig Rixford. 1998. *Lessons Learned from the History of Social Indicators.* San Francisco: Redefining Progress.

Coleman-Jensen, Alisha, Matthew P. Rabbitt, Christian A. Gregory, and Anita Singh. 2021. *Household Food Security in the United States in 2020.* ERR-298, U.S. Department of Agriculture, Economic Research Service.

Conroy, Frank. 1993. *Body & Soul.* Kindle edition. New York: Houghton Mifflin.

Courtright, John F., William H. Acton, Michael L. Frazier, and J. Walter Lane. 1988. "Test and Evaluation Effects of 'Workarounds' on Perceptions of Problem Importance during Operational Test." Human Factors and Ergonomics Society Annual Meeting Proceedings: Test and Evaluation, 1150–1153.

Crosby, Ned, Janet M. Kelley, and Paul Schaefer. 1986. "Citizen Panels: A New Approach to Citizen Participation." *Public Administration Review* 46 (2): 170–178.

Dahl, Robert A. 1967. "The City in the Future of Democracy." *American Political Science Review* 41 (4): 953–970.

DeFilippis, James. 2007. "Erasing the Community in Order to Save It? Reconstructing Community and Property in Community Development." In *Neighbourhood Renewal and Housing Markets: Community Engagement in the US and UK,* edited by Harris Beider. Malden, MA: Blackwell.

Detienne, Marcel, and Jean-Pierre Vernant. 1978. *Cunning Intelligence in Greek Culture and Society.* Sussex: Harvester.

Dicke, Lisa A., and J. Steven Ott. 1999. "Public Agency Accountability in Human Services Contracting." *Public Productivity and Management Review* 22 (4): 502–516.

DiIulio, John J., Jr. 2007. *Godly Republic: A Centrist Blueprint for America's Faith-Based Future*. Berkeley: University of California Press.

Dolbeare, Kenneth M., and Murray J. Edelman. 1985. *American Politics: Policies, Power, and Change*. Lexington, MA: D. C. Heath.

Dunne, Joseph. 1993. *Back to the Rough Ground: "Phronesis" and "Techne" in Modern Philosophy and in Aristotle*. Notre Dame, IN: University of Notre Dame Press.

Dye, Thomas R., and Harmon Zeigler. 1987. *The Irony of Democracy: An Uncommon Introduction to American Politics*. Monterey, CA: Brooks/Cole.

Dzur, Albert W. 2008. *Democratic Professionalism: Citizen Participation and the Reconstruction of Professional Ethics, Identity, and Practice*. University Park, PA: Penn State University Press.

———. 2019. *Democracy Inside: Participatory Innovation in Unlikely Places*. New York: Oxford University Press.

Eckstein, Barbara, and James A. Throgmorton. 2003. *Story and Sustainability: Planning, Practice, and Possibility for American Cities*. Cambridge, MA: MIT Press.

Edwards, Michael. 2010. *Small Change: Why Business Won't Save the World*. San Francisco: Berrett-Koehler.

Eikenberry, Angela M., and Roseanne Mirabella. 2018. "Extreme Philanthropy: Philanthrocapitalism, Effective Altruism, and the Discourse of Neoliberalism." *PS*, January: 43–47.

Elbow, Peter. 1986. *Embracing Contraries: Explorations in Learning and Teaching*. New York: Oxford University Press.

Eliasoph, Nina. 2011. *Making Volunteers: Civic Life after Welfare's End*. Princeton, NJ: Princeton University Press.

———. 2014. "Measuring the Grassroots: Puzzles of Cultivating the Grassroots from the Top Down." *Sociological Quarterly* 55 (3): 467–492. Available at https://doi.org/10.1111/tsq.12063.

Ellul, Jacques. 1964. *The Technological Society*. New York: Vintage Books.

———. 2016. *Presence in the Modern World*. Translated by Lisa Richmond. Eugene, OR: Cascade Books.

Fehler-Cabral, Giannina, Jennifer James, Hallie Preskill, and Meg Long. 2016. "The Art and Science of Place-Based Philanthropy: Themes from a National Convening." *Foundation Review* 8 (2): 84–96.

Ferneley, Elaine H., and Polly Sobreperez. 2006. "Resist, Comply, or Workaround? An Examination of Different Facets of User Engagement with Information Systems." *European Journal of Information Systems* 15: 345–356.

Fishkin, James S. 1991. *Democracy and Deliberation: New Directions for Democratic Reform*. New Haven, CT: Yale University Press.

Follett, Mary Parker. 1992. "The Giving of Orders." In *Classics of Public Administration*, 3rd ed., edited by Jay M. Shafritz and Albert C. Hyde, 66–74. Pacific Grove, CA: Brooks/Cole.

Forester, John. 1999. *The Deliberative Practitioner: Encouraging Participatory Planning Processes*. Cambridge, MA: MIT Press.

Foucault, Michel. 2000. "The Subject and Power." In *Power*, vol. 3 of *Essential Works of Foucault, 1954–1984*, edited by James D. Faubion, 347–348. New York: New Press.

Fredrickson, H. George. 2000a. "Lessons from Government Reform." *PA Times* 23 (7): 8.

———. 2000b. "Measuring Performance in Theory and Practice." *PA Times* 23 (8): 8.

Friedman, Mark. 2005. *Trying Hard Is Not Enough: How to Produce Measurable Improvements for Customers and Communities*. Victoria, Canada: Trafford.

Gardner, Sidney L. 2005. *Cities, Counties, Kids, and Families: The Essential Role of Local Government*. Lanham, MD: University Press of America.

Giloth, Robert, ed. 2004. *Workforce Intermediaries for the Twenty-First Century*. Philadelphia: Temple University Press.

———. 2019. "Philanthropy and Economic Development: New Roles and Strategies." *Economic Development Quarterly* 33 (3): 159–168.

Glazer, Nathan. 1988. *The Limits of Social Policy*. Cambridge, MA: Harvard University Press.

Goldrich, Daniel. 1986. "Democracy and Energy Planning: The Pacific Northwest as Prototype." *Environmental Review* 10 (3): 199–214.

Gore, Albert. 1993. *From Red Tape to Results: Creating a Government That Works Better and Costs Less: Report of the National Performance Review*. Washington, DC: U.S. Government Printing Office.

Gronbjerg, Kristen A., and Steven Rathgeb Smith. 2021. *The Changing Dynamic of Government-Nonprofit Relationships*. Cambridge: Cambridge University Press.

Habermas, Jurgen. 1991. *The Philosophical Discourses of Modernity*. Cambridge, MA: MIT Press.

Hacker, Jacob S. 2004. "Privatizing Risk without Privatizing the Welfare State: The Hidden Politics of Social Policy Retrenchment in the United States." *American Political Science Review* 98 (2): 243–260.

Harder+Company. 2004. Civic Engagement in California: An Evaluation of the Civic Engagement Project for Children and Families. Prepared for the Civic Engagement Project for Children and Families Steering Committee.

Harmon, Michael M. 1995. *Responsibility as Paradox: A Critique of Rational Discourse on Government*. Thousand Oaks, CA: Sage.

Hart, Maureen. 1999. *Guide to Sustainable Community Indicators*. North Andover, MA: Hart Environmental Data.

Harwood, Richard C. 2021. *Unleashed: A Proven Way Communities Can Spread Change and Make Hope Real for All*. Kettering, OH: Kettering Foundation.

Hess, David J. 2007. *Alternative Pathways in Science and Industry: Activism, Innovation, and the Environment in an Era of Globalization*. Cambridge, MA: MIT Press.

Horne, Christopher S., John K. Brock, J. Kenzie Freeman, and Holly S. Odell. 2021. "Conceptualizing and Measuring the Promotion of Nonprofit Organizations' Evidence Use by U.S. Social Service Funding Programs." *Journal of Public and Nonprofit Affairs* 7 (2): 240–263.

Horwitt, Sanford D. 1989. *Let Them Call Me Rebel: Saul Alinsky, His Life and Legacy.* New York: Knopf.

Hupe, Peter L., and Michael J. Hill. 2006. "The Three Action Levels of Governance: Re-framing the Policy Process beyond the Stages Model." In *Handbook of Public Policy*, edited by B. Guy Peters and Jon Pierre, 13–30. Thousand Oaks, CA: Sage.

Hyatt, Susan Britt. 2001. "From Citizen to Volunteer: Neoliberal Governance and the Erasure of Poverty." In *The New Poverty Studies: The Ethnography of Power, Politics and Impoverished People in the United States*, edited by Judith Goode and Jeff Maskovsky, 201–235. New York: New York University Press.

Immerwahr, Daniel. 2015. *Thinking Small: The United States and the Lure of Community Development.* Cambridge, MA: Harvard University Press.

James, Oliver, Asmus Leth Olsen, Donald P. Moynihan, and Gregg G. Van Ryzin. 2020. *Behavioral Public Performance: How People Make Sense of Government Metrics.* Cambridge: Cambridge University Press.

Johnson, Julie K., Stephen H. Miller, and Sheldon D. Horowitz. 2008. "Systems-Based Practice: Improving the Safety and Quality of Patient Care by Recognizing and Improving the Systems in Which We Work." In *Advances in Patient Safety: New Directions and Alternative Approaches*, vol. 2, *Culture and Redesign*, edited by Kerm Henriksen, James B. Battles, Margaret A. Keyes, and Mary L. Grady. Rockville, MD: Agency for Healthcare Research and Quality. Available at https://www.ncbi.nlm.nih.gov/books/NBK43731/.

Karpowitz, Christopher F., and Jane Mansbridge. 2005. "Disagreement and Consensus: The Need for Dynamic Updating in Public Deliberation." *Journal of Public Deliberation* 1 (1): article 2. Available at https://www.publicdeliberation.net/jpd/vol1/iss1/art2.

Kearns, Kevin P. 1996. *Managing for Accountability: Preserving Public Trust in Public and Nonprofit Organizations.* San Francisco: Jossey-Bass.

Keith-Lucas, Alan. 1972. *Giving and Taking Help.* Chapel Hill: University of North Carolina Press.

Kemmis, Daniel. 1990. *Community and the Politics of Place.* Norman: University of Oklahoma Press.

Kennedy, Sheila Seuss, and Wolfgang Bielefeld. 2006. *Charitable Choice at Work: Evaluating Faith-Based Jobs Programs in the States.* Washington, DC: Georgetown University Press.

Kettl, Donald F. 1980. *Managing Community Development in the New Federalism.* New York: Praeger.

———. 2000. "The Transformation of Governance: Globalization, Devolution, and the Role of Government." *Public Administration Review* 60: 488–497.

———. 2006. "Managing Boundaries in American Administration: The Collaboration Imperative." *Public Administration Review* 66: 10–19.

———. 2015. *The Transformation of Governance: Public Administration for the 21st Century*. Baltimore: Johns Hopkins University Press.

Kohl-Arenas, Erica. 2015. *The Self-Help Myth: How Philanthropy Fails to Alleviate Poverty*. Berkeley: University of California Press.

Kollock, Deborah Hansen, Lynette Flage, Scott Shazdon, Nathan Paine, and Lorie Higgins. 2012. "Ripple Effect Mapping: A 'Radiant' Way to Capture Program Impacts." *Journal of Extension* 50 (5): article number 5TOT6. Available at https://archives.joe.org/joe/2012october/pdf/JOE_v50_5tt6.pdf.

Lasch, Christopher. 1984. *The Minimal Self: Psychic Survival in Troubled Times*. New York: W. W. Norton.

Lee, Caroline W. 2007. "Is There a Place for Private Conversation in Public Dialogue? Comparing Stakeholder Assessments of Informal Communication in Collaborative Regional Planning." *American Journal of Sociology* 113 (1): 41–96.

Levin, Martin A., and Mary Bryna Sanger. 1994. *Making Government Work: How Entrepreneurial Executives Turn Bright Ideas into Real Results*. San Francisco: Jossey-Bass.

Levine, Caroline. 2015. *Forms: Whole, Rhythm, Hierarchy, Network*. Princeton, NJ: Princeton University Press.

Li, Tanya Murray. 2006. "Neo-liberal Strategies of Government through Community: The Social Development Program of the World Bank in Indonesia." International Law and Justice Working Paper 2, 1–35, Global Administrative Law Series. New York: New York University School of Law.

Lilienthal, David E. 1944. *Democracy on the March*. New York: Harper Collins.

Lindblom, Charles E. 1959. "The Science of Muddling Through." *Public Administration Review* 19 (2): 79–88.

———. 1979. "Still Muddling, Not Yet Through." *Public Administration Review* 39 (6): 517–526.

Lipsky, Michael. 1980. *Street-Level Bureaucracy: Dilemmas of the Individual in Public Service*. New York: Russell Sage Foundation.

MacIntyre, Alasdair. 2007. *After Virtue: A Study in Moral Theory*. 3rd ed. Notre Dame, IN: University of Notre Dame Press.

Marquez, Xavier. 2012. "Spaces of Appearance and Spaces of Surveillance." *Polity* 44 (1): 6–31.

Matthews, David. 2014. "Afterthoughts." *Kettering Review* 32 (1): 55–58.

Matthews, David, and Noel McAfee. 2003. *Making Choices Together: The Power of Public Deliberation*. Kettering, OH: National Issues Forum Institute.

Mazmanian, Daniel A., and Paul Sabatier. 1989. *Implementation and Public Policy*. Lanham, NY: University Press of America.

McGee, Rosemary. 2002. "Participating in Development." In *Development Theory and Practice: Critical Perspectives*, edited by Uma Kothari and Martin Minogue, 92–116. Hampshire: Palgrave.

McIvor, David W. 2020. "Toward a Critical Theory of Collaborative Governance." *Administrative Theory and Practice* 42 (4): 501–516.

McKnight, John. 1995. *The Careless Society: Community and Its Counterfeits.* New York: Basic Books.

Meagher, Kelsey D., David C. Campbell, and Edward S. Spang. 2022. "Understanding the Impacts of the COVID-19 Pandemic on California's Emergency Food System." Davis: University of California, Davis Food Loss and Waste Collaborative.

Miller, Denise C. 2009. "Faith-Based Organization Welcomes Women Back Home into the Community." *Family and Community Health* 32 (4): 298–308.

Miller, Mike. 1978. *The Ideology of the Community Organizing Movement.* San Francisco: Organizing Training Center.

Mills, C. Wright. 1959. *The Sociological Imagination.* New York: Oxford University Press.

Morgan, Douglas, Kelly G. Bacon, Ron Bunch, Charles D. Cameron, and Robert Deis. 1996. "What Middle Managers Do in Local Government: Stewardship of the Public Trust and the Limits of Reinventing Government." *Public Administration Review* 56 (4): 359–366.

Morgan, Gareth. 1986. *Images of Organization.* Newbury Park, CA: Sage.

Moynihan, Donald P. 2008. *The Dynamics of Performance Management.* Washington, DC: Georgetown University Press.

Muller, Jerry. 2018. *The Tyranny of Metrics.* Princeton, NJ: Princeton University Press.

Murphey, David A. 1999. "Presenting Community-Level Data in an 'Outcomes and Indicators' Framework: Lessons from Vermont's Experience." *Public Administration Review* 59 (1): 76–82.

Neblo, Michael A., and Jeremy L. Wallace. 2021. "A Plague on Politics? The Covid Crisis, Expertise, and the Future of Legitimation." *American Political Science Review* 115 (4): 1524–1529.

Neustadt, Richard E., and Ernst R. May. 1986. *Thinking in Time: The Uses of History for Decision Makers.* New York: Free Press.

Newcomer, Kathryn E., ed. 1997. *Using Performance Measurement to Improve Public and Nonprofit Programs.* San Francisco: Jossey-Bass.

Newfield, Christopher, Ann Alexandrova, and Stephen John, eds. 2022. *Limits of the Numerical.* Chicago: University of Chicago Press.

North Central Regional Center for Rural Development. 1997. *Working toward Community Goals: Helping Communities Succeed.* Workbook for Community Action Teams collaborating with the Rural Community Assistance Program of the USDA Forest Service.

Office of Governor Gavin Newsom. 2020. "Governor Newsom Deploys California National Guard to Help Distribute Food at Food Banks and Protect California's Most Vulnerable." California Governor. March 21, 2020. https://www.gov.ca.gov/2020/03/20/governor-newsom-deploys-california-national-guard-to-help-distribute-food-at-food-banks-protect-californias-most-vulnerable/.

O'Leary, Rosemary. 2010. "Guerilla Employees: Should Managers Nurture, Tolerate, or Terminate Them?" *Public Administration Review* 70 (1): 8–19.

O'Leary, Rosemary, Beth Gazley, Michael McGuire, and Lisa Blomgren Bingham. 2009. "Public Managers in Collaboration." In *The Collaborative Public Manager*, edited by Rosemary O'Leary and Lisa Blomgren Bingham, 1–12. Washington, DC: Georgetown University Press.

Ostrom, Elinor. 2002. "Policy Analysis in the Future of Good Societies." *Good Society* 11 (1): 42–48.

———. 2010. "Beyond Markets and States: Polycentric Governance of Complex Economic Systems." *American Economic Review* 100 (3): 641–672.

Patton, Michael Quinn. 2002. *Qualitative Research and Evaluation Methods*. Thousand Oaks, CA: Sage.

———. 2011. *Developmental Evaluation: Applying Complexity Concepts to Enhance Innovation and Use*. New York: Guilford.

Peters, Scott J. 2010. *Democracy and Higher Education: Traditions and Stories of Civic Engagement*. East Lansing: Michigan State University Press.

Peters, Scott J., Theodore R. Alter, and Timothy J. Shaffer. 2010. "Hot Passion and Cool Judgment: Relating Reason and Emotion in Democratic Politics." Kettering Foundation, *Connections*, 15–17.

Pierce, Gregory. 1984. *Activism That Makes Sense*. Ramsay, NJ: Paulist.

Pierre, Jon, and B. Guy Peters. 2021. *Advanced Introduction to Governance*. Cheltenham, U.K.: Edward Elgar.

Porter, Theodore M. 1995. *Trust in Numbers: The Pursuit of Objectivity in Science and Public Life*. Princeton, NJ: Princeton University Press.

Posner, Paul. 2009. "A Public Administration Education for the Third-Party Governance Era: Reclaiming Leadership of the Field." In *The Collaborative Public Manager*, edited by Rosemary O'Leary and Lisa Blomgren Bingham, 233–254. Washington, DC: Georgetown University Press.

Pressman, Jeffrey L., and Aaron Wildavsky. 1979. *Implementation: How Great Expectations in Washington Are Dashed in Oakland*. Berkeley, University of California Press.

Putnam, Robert D. 2020. *The Upswing: How America Came Together a Century Ago and How We Can Do It Again*. New York: Simon and Schuster.

Radin, Beryl A. 2006. *Challenging the Performance Movement: Accountability, Complexity, and Democratic Values*. Washington, DC: Georgetown University Press.

Redefining Progress. 1997. *The Community Indicators Handbook: Measuring Progress toward Healthy and Sustainable Communities*. San Francisco: Redefining Progress.

Risser, Paul G. 1995. "The Status of the Science Examining Ecotones." *BioScience* 45 (5): 318–325.

Rose, Nikolas. 1996. "Governing 'Advanced' Liberal Democracies." In *Foucault and Political Reason*, edited by Andrew Barry, Thomas Osborne, and Nikolas Rose, 37–64. Chicago: University of Chicago Press.

Saidel, Judith Richman. 1991. "Resource Interdependence: The Relationship between State Agencies and Nonprofit Organizations." *Public Administration Review* 51 (6): 543–553.

Salamon, Lester M. 1995. *Partners in Public Service*. Baltimore: Johns Hopkins University Press.

———, ed. 2002. *The Tools of Government: A Guide to the New Governance*. New York: Oxford University Press.

Sawicki, David S., and Patrice Flynn. 1996. "Neighborhood Indicators: A Review of the Literature and an Assessment of Conceptual and Methodological Issues." *Journal of the American Planning Association* 62 (2): 165–183.

Schon, Donald. 1983. *The Reflective Practitioner*. New York: Basic Books.

Schorr, Lisbeth B. 1989. *Within Our Reach: Breaking the Cycle of Disadvantage*. New York: Anchor Books.

———. 1997. *Common Purpose: Strengthening Families and Neighborhoods to Rebuild America*. New York: Anchor Books.

Schwandt, Thomas A. 2008. "Educating for Intelligent Belief in Evaluation." *American Journal of Evaluation* 29 (2): 139–150.

Schwartz, Barry, and Kenneth Sharpe. 2010. *Practical Wisdom: The Right Way to Do the Right Thing*. New York: Riverhead Books.

Scott, James C. 1990. *Domination and the Arts of Resistance: Hidden Transcripts*. New Haven, CT: Yale University Press.

———. 1998. *Seeing like a State: How Certain Schemes to Improve the Human Condition Have Failed*. New Haven, CT: Yale University Press.

Scriven, Michael, ed. 1993. "Hard-Won Lessons in Program Evaluation." *New Directions for Evaluation* 58: 1–103.

Seligman, Martin E. P. 1975. *Helplessness: On Development, Depression, and Death*. New York: W. H. Freedman.

Sennett, Richard. 1974. *The Fall of Public Man: On the Social Psychology of Capitalism*. New York: Vintage Books.

———. 2003. *Respect in a World of Inequality*. New York: W. W. Norton.

———. 2006. *The Culture of the New Capitalism*. New Haven, CT: Yale University Press.

———. 2008. *The Craftsman*. New Haven, CT: Yale University Press.

———. 2012. *Together: The Rituals, Pleasures and Politics of Cooperation*. New Haven, CT: Yale University Press.

Shapin, Steven. 2010. *Never Pure: Historical Studies of Science as if It Was Produced by People with Bodies, Situated in Time, Space, Culture, and Society, and Struggling for Credibility and Authority*. Baltimore: Johns Hopkins University Press.

Singer, Peter. 2015. *The Most Good You Can Do: How Effective Altruism Is Changing Ideas about Living Ethically*. New Haven, CT: Yale University Press.

Smith, Steven Rathgeb, and Michael Lipsky. 1995. *Nonprofits for Hire: The Welfare State in the Age of Contracting*. Cambridge, MA: Harvard University Press.

Sokolow, Al, and Peter Detwiler. 2001. "State-Local Relations in California." In *Home Rule in America: A Fifty State Handbook*, edited by Dale A. Krane, 58–68. Washington, DC: Congressional Quarterly.

Soss, Joe, Richard C. Fording, and Sanford F. Schram. 2011. *Disciplining the Poor: Neoliberal Paternalism and the Persistent Power of Race.* Chicago: University of Chicago Press.

Stivers, Camilla. 2000. *Bureau Men and Settlement Women: Constructing Public Administration in the Progressive Era.* Lawrence: University of Kansas Press.

Stone, Clarence, Marion Orr, and Donn Worgs. 2006. "The Flight of the Bumblebee: Why Reform Is Difficult but Not Impossible." *Perspectives on Politics* 4 (3): 529–546.

Storing, Herbert J. 1980. "American Statesmanship: Old and New." In *Bureaucrats, Policy Analysts, Statesman: Who Leads?* edited by Robert A. Goodwin, 88–113. Washington, DC: American Enterprise Institute.

Taylor, Charles. 1991. *The Ethics of Authenticity.* Cambridge, MA: Harvard University Press.

———. 2007. *A Secular Age.* Cambridge, MA: Belknap Press of Harvard University Press.

Taylor, Frederick W. 1911. *The Principles of Scientific Management.* New York: Harper and Brothers.

Thompson, Dennis. 2008. "Deliberative Democratic Theory and Empirical Political Science." *Annual Review of Political Science* 11: 497–520.

Tocqueville, Alexis de. 1945. *Democracy in America.* Vol. 2. New York: Vintage Books.

United Way of America. 1996. *Measuring Program Outcomes: A Practical Approach.* Alexandria, VA: United Way of America.

USDA Agricultural Marketing Service. 2021. "USDA Farmers to Families Food Box." Available at https://www.ams.usda.gov/selling-food-to-usda/farmers-to-families-food-box.

Vestal, Katherine. 2008. "Nursing and the Art of the Workaround." *Nurse Leader* 6 (4): 8–9.

Warren, Mark R. 2001. *Dry Bones Rattling: Community Building to Revitalize American Democracy.* Princeton, NJ: Princeton University Press.

Weeks, Edward C. 2000. "The Practice of Deliberative Democracy: Results from Four Large-Scale Trials." *Public Administration Review* 60 (4): 360–372.

Wells, Miriam J. 1996. *Strawberry Fields: Politics, Class, and Work in California Agriculture.* Ithaca, NY: Cornell University Press.

Wholey, Joseph S., and Harry P. Hatry. 1992. "The Case for Performance Monitoring." *Public Administration Review* 52 (6): 604–610.

Wiebe, Robert H. 1995. *Self-Rule: A Cultural History of American Democracy.* Chicago: University of Chicago Press.

Wilson, Woodrow. 1887. "The Study of Administration." *Political Science Quarterly* 2 (2): 197–222.

Wineburg, Robert J. 2001. *A Limited Partnership: The Politics of Religion, Welfare, and Social Service*. New York: Columbia University Press.

Wolch, Jennifer. 1990. *The Shadow State: Government and Voluntary Sector in Transition*. Washington, DC: Foundation Center.

Wolfe, Alan. 1989. *Whose Keeper? Social Science and Moral Obligation*. Berkeley: University of California Press.

Wuthnow, Robert. 2004. *Saving America? Faith-Based Services and the Future of Civil Society*. Princeton, NJ: Princeton University Press.

Zacka, Bernardo. 2017. *When the State Meets the Street: Public Service and Moral Agency*. Cambridge, MA: Belknap Press of Harvard University Press.

Index

processes in, 132–137; emotions in, 127, 136–137; factors affecting success in, 116–128; feedback in (*see* Feedback loops in results accountability); flexible approach to, 55–57; as form or practice, 142–144; goal clarity in, 116, 117t, 118, 127; in governance reforms, 16, 26; leadership of hidden heroes in, 22–23; learning in, 116, 117t, 128, 138–142; logic models in, 18, 94, 128; nature of evaluative assessment in, 22; for nonprofit organizations, 26, 39, 41, 94, 96; performance standards in (*see* Performance standards); program-centric perspective in, 22, 93, 99–100, 106, 146t; redeeming promise of, 115–144; scale in (*see* Scale in outcomes assessment); technical assistance and training on, 94; in welfare reform, 38–39, 41, 42, 74; and "Why?" question on results, 19; workarounds in, 80–85, 87; in workforce development programs, 51, 54–57, 72, 74, 80–85, 97–99; in youth program, 3–4, 5

Results attributions, 92–112; in codetermination work, 93, 99–106, 146t; in network dynamics, 92, 94–99, 146t; time frame in, 93, 106–112

Rose, Nikolas, 14, 28

Rules, 11, 12, 22, 71–88, 146t; in codetermination work, 105–106; consistency and fairness in, 87, 146t; and fit of policy to place, 79–85, 146t; on front-door services and backdoor accounting, 79, 85, 146t; local discretion in, 12, 80, 83, 87–88, 146t; in service integration, 76, 85–86, 146t; as starting points for negotiations, 79, 84, 87, 146t; Taylor on, 156–157; workarounds for (*see* Workarounds)

Rural areas: impact of welfare reform in, 43; workforce development programs in, 79–86

Salvation Army, 43

Sanctions: in school attendance program, 25, 137; in workforce development programs, 72, 73–74, 102

Scale in outcomes assessment, 11, 22, 89–112, 146t; in codetermination work, 93, 99–106, 146t; in collaborative programs, 95; in community-scale indicators (*see* Community-scale indicators); in Humboldt County economic development project, 96–97, 120; in network dynamics, 92, 93, 94–99, 146t; in PlacerGROWN, 129; in program-centric perspective, 22, 93, 99–100, 128–132, 146t; project-level outcomes in, 96; time frame in, 11, 93, 106–112, 146t

Schon, Donald, 172n2

School attendance: data collection and analysis on, 117t; health issues affecting, 136, 174n8; in Merced County project (*see* Merced County Attendance Project); metrics indicating success in, 25; sanctions in, 25, 137; in youth workforce development program, 6

Schorr, Lisbeth, 30

Schwandt, Thomas, 141

Scientific standards in outcome data, 119, 120

Scott, James, 21, 28

Seeing Like a State (Scott), 21

Self-esteem: in codetermination work, 100, 103, 130; in teen pregnancy project, 124

Self-sufficiency: service integration for, 85; in workforce development programs, 55, 82

Sennett, Richard, 174n9

David C. Campbell is Emeritus Professor of Cooperative Extension in the Department of Human Ecology at the University of California, Davis.

Printed and bound by CPI Group (UK) Ltd, Croydon, CR0 4YY

01/04/2024